100 THINGS TO DO IN DAYTONA BEACH BEFORE YOU DIE

DEDICATION

To my wife, Christina, for her love and support.

Reedy Press
PO Box 5131
St. Louis, MO 63139, USA
reedypress.com

Library of Congress Control Number: 2025948692

ISBN: 9781681066295

Design by Jill Halpin

Cover photo courtesy of Robert Redd

Unless otherwise noted, all photos are courtesy of the author or are believed to be in the public domain.

Printed in the United States of America
26 27 28 29 30   5 4 3 2 1

100 THINGS TO DO IN DAYTONA BEACH BEFORE YOU DIE

•••••••••••••••••••••••••

ROBERT REDD

CONTENTS

Music and Entertainment

Sports and Recreation

Culture and History

Shopping and Fashion

Barberville Pioneer Settlement

PREFACE

The reputation of Daytona Beach has been built upon four basic pillars: auto racing, bike week, spring break, and the hard-packed sands of the "World's Most Famous Beach." Today, three of the four are still major components of the local economic engine. Spring break, while still accounting for a level of tourism, is a far different animal than the out-of-control partying broadcast across the country during the heady days when MTV invaded the town.

Since the year 2000, Daytona Beach has seen an increase in population of around 33 percent, not including the surrounding areas of Ormond Beach, Holly Hill, Port Orange, and New Smyrna Beach. Why do so many people move to Daytona Beach, and why do millions of visitors flock to the town?

The weather is the obvious answer for many. Yes, it gets very hot and very humid. Hurricanes are a yearly concern. During the summer months, carry your umbrella because the afternoon rain is coming. But when late fall and winter arrive, the temperatures are moderate, and for those used to shoveling snow, it's a welcome change.

While racing, motorcycles, and the beach are still important, Daytona Beach offers so much more. Location is a prime factor, with the larger cities of Orlando, Jacksonville, Tampa, and even Miami all being within a reasonable driving distance.

But you don't have to leave the area to enjoy "big city" life. Daytona Beach offers professional baseball; high quality history, art, and science museums; outdoor activities; multiple shopping venues; symphony performances; college football; live theater; and every type of restaurant imaginable.

This book only scratches the surface on what there is to do in the Daytona Beach area. I hope that it provides a starting point for visitors and turns locals onto a few places they may have missed. For the businesses mentioned, if I have helped bring people to your doors, I have achieved my goal.

ACKNOWLEDGMENTS

Writing is often seen as a solitary activity, and while the act itself is lonely—just the author, a keyboard, and a flashing cursor—there is more to it. There are always people behind the scenes.

First, I always have to thank my friend Jim Schmidt, who encouraged me years ago when I was starting on my first book. He guided me through the query process and helped polish the manuscript while providing suggestions and guidance along the way. Every writer needs a Jim Schmidt in their life.

I want to thank the folks at Reedy Press, particularly Alex McPherson who saw value in the book idea and helped bring me into the Reedy Press family.

Thank you to the Halifax Area Advertising Authority, locally known as HAAA, and the Daytona Beach Area Convention and Visitors Bureau for all the tireless and often thankless promotional efforts you provide to continue bringing the seemingly endless stream of visitors to our area.

My mother has been a continued support through my writing journey.

Hill's Chicken and Waffles

FOOD AND DRINK

1

WITNESS CANDYMAKERS
AT WORK AT ANGELL & PHELPS

When Riddell Angell and Cora Phelps started their candy company in 1925 on Mackinac Island, Michigan, they had no intention of moving to Daytona Beach. World War II, however, led to a change in plans, and the business partners headed south, where the business has been for almost 100 years.

Get your free samples, find a spot at the large cottage windows, and watch experienced candymakers make delicious treats the old-fashioned way. Don't leave without a box of caramels, or maybe pecan honeybees. The chocolate-covered pretzels and potato chips are visitor favorites. Take home a Barker's Dozen for your best friend. Covered in white chocolate, with no cocoa, these are perfect treats for your four-legged companion. Want to surprise your friends and family back home with a delicious treat? Angell & Phelps will ship for you. Just ask.

154 S Beach St., 386-252-6531
angellandphelps.com

TIP

You may be told by some locals, or see on old web pages, a recommendation to take the tour of the candy factory. Unfortunately, Angell & Phelps no longer offers such a tour. Visitors can, however, see candymakers hard at work through the large windows in the store. It's a sight young and old enjoy!

2

MAKE BREAKFAST
AT THE OLD SUGAR MILL PANCAKE HOUSE

A delight for the young and young at heart, the Old Sugar Mill Pancake House, located inside De Leon Springs State Park, gives you the opportunity to make your own pancakes however you like them. You pour the batter yourself at a griddle right at your table. Located in a 100-year-old replica of an 1830s sugar mill, Old Sugar Mill will make you feel like you've been transported back in time. Want your pancakes large? Done. Silver dollar sized? No problem. Fruit? Of course. Chocolate chips? Add them in. It's all you can eat, so let your imagination run wild. Not in the mood for pancakes? Order from the regular menu, which features breakfast and lunch items.

After eating your fill, take in beautiful De Leon Springs State Park. Go for a swim, take an Eco Boat Tour, or maybe just stroll the nature trails. You might see alligators, bald eagles, turtles, manatees, deer, or bobcats—wild Florida will always amaze you.

601 Ponce Deleon Blvd., De Leon Springs, 855-980-2665
https://www.floridastateparks.org/parks-and-trails/de-leon-springs-state-park/old-sugar-mill-pancake-house

TIP

If you want breakfast at the Old Sugar Mill Pancake House, make your reservation as soon as you arrive at the park. This is a very popular family activity, and wait times can be quite long, particularly on weekends and during the summer.

3

ENJOY SOUTHERN HOSPITALITY

AT ROSE VILLA SOUTHERN TABLE AND BAR

The Rose Villa building began life as a small adjunct building to the much larger Ormond Hotel, built by Standard Oil tycoon and railroad magnate Henry Flagler. Over the years the building served as a ticket office for the Florida East Coast Railway, as a hotel bearing several different names, and even as a real estate office before Bill Jones purchased the property in 2007, turning it into the gem diners find today. You can dine on elevated southern staples such as fried green tomatoes, pork belly, bourbon barbecue pork chops, southern fried chicken, shrimp and grits, jambalaya, and more. Are you wanting a drink? Head upstairs where you'll find Whiskey at the Rose, a traditional speakeasy, offering an incredible lineup of high-end bourbons and mixed drinks made from the finest ingredients. With only eight seats, you'll feel like you're in an exclusive club. Make reservations at Rose Villa for your next special occasion.

43 W Granada Blvd., Ormond Beach, 386-615-7673
rosevillaormondbeach.com

TIP

Try to dine in the different themed areas, including the beautiful front porch or maybe the Theodore Roosevelt Room.

ENJOY OKTOBERFEST
AT MR. DUNDERBAK'S

A Daytona Beach staple since 1975, Mr. Dunderbak's has a well-deserved reputation for serving only the finest Bavarian and German deli foods. If you are looking for a true Reuben sandwich or traditional schnitzel, Mr. Dunderbak's should be your Daytona Beach destination. Sandwiches made with the highest-quality deli meats are always a favorite. If you would rather stick with American foods, a variety of burgers and chicken dishes are available.

Mr. Dunderbak's doesn't just serve meals. It offers an assortment of meats, cheeses, sauces, olives, teas, and coffees. Be sure to pick up the potato pancake mix for a delicious home meal. And what's a German restaurant without beer? Draft, cans, and bottles of beers and ciders you won't find at the grocery store await.

In 2023, original owner Ted Teschner and his family retired after being in the restaurant business for 47 years. The new owners, father and son Doug and Matt Martin, continue the legacy of great food and service created by the Teschner family.

Volusia Mall
1700 W International Speedway Blvd., #210, 386-258-1600
facebook.com/p/Mr-Dunderbaks-100063505063319

SAMPLE CRAFT BEER
AT ORMOND GARAGE

Relive racing history at the Ormond Garage. Ormond Beach can trace its beach-racing roots to the early 1900s. Henry Flagler built the original Ormond Garage in 1904 to accommodate racers and eliminate clutter on the grounds of his Ormond Hotel. Sadly, the original Ormond Garage burned to the ground in 1976. Now, decades later, the new version of the Ormond Garage keeps the legacy alive, albeit in a different garage location. Today, visitors to the Ormond Garage can choose from burgers, tacos, sandwiches, and vegetarian options while enjoying the surroundings, hearkening back to the days when mechanics tried to gain every 10th of a mile per hour out of their cars. Wash down your meal with a freshly-crafted, in-house brewed beer. Whether you are a fan of ale, IPA, stout, or Mexican lager, the Ormond Garage is brewing it up and serving it ice-cold. A limited selection of spirits and wine is also available.

48 W Granada Blvd., Ormond Beach, 386-492-7981
ormondgarage.beer

DISCOVER YOUR NEW FAVORITE LOCAL BEERS AND SPIRITS

Copper Bottom Craft Distillery

998 N Beach St., Holly Hill, 386-267-5104
copperbottomspirits.com

Drunken Duck Brewing Company

101 2nd St., Unit 401, Holly Hill, 386-506-1788
drunkenduckbrewingcompany.com

Dunes Brewing

59 Dunlawton Ave., Unit 102, Port Orange, 386-872-4007
dunesbrewing.com

New Smyrna Beach Brewing Company

143 Canal St., New Smyrna Beach, 386-957-3802
newsmyrnabeachbrewery.com

Persimmon Hollow Brewing Co.

111 W Georgia Ave., DeLand, 386-873-7350
persimmonhollowbrewing.com

Sugar Works Distillery

214 N Orange St., New Smyrna Beach 386-463-0120
sugarworksdistillery.com

Typsy Unicorn's Brewing

2140 S Riverside Dr., Unit 19/20, Edgewater, 386-444-3047
typsyunicornsbrewing.com

6

TAKE IN THE VIEWS
FROM TOP OF DAYTONA

Located on the 29th floor of the second-tallest building in Daytona Beach, Top of Daytona offers diners stunning ocean and river views. Peck Plaza, originally constructed in 1974 by Edwin W. Peck Sr., is primarily a residential condominium building. Directly facing the Atlantic Ocean, with amenities such as a large swimming pool and several tennis courts, Peck Plaza draws residents and out-of-town guests with prime views, a convenient location, and a restaurant offering delicious food and top-notch local entertainment. If you love seafood, you'll have a hard time deciding between the changing featured dishes such as the panko-and-parmesan-crusted red snapper, seared scallops, grouper, and more. Steaks, chicken, and lamb are on the menu along with vegetarian options. Be sure to order one of the best mixed drinks in the Daytona Beach area at the center bar.

Top of Daytona is the basis of one of the longest-held myths associated with Daytona Beach. Many locals will tell you that Top of Daytona used to rotate, allowing diners to see all the surrounding area from high above. This myth has been dispelled many times by Edwin W. Peck Sr.

2625 S Atlantic Ave., 29th Floor, Daytona Beach Shores
386-310-7849
facebook.com/topofdaytona29

7

HAVE YOUR EGGS ANY STYLE
AT THE CRACKED EGG DINER

Poached, scrambled, omelets, Benedict, sunny-side up, or however you prefer, brothers Chris and Kevin Purucker will make sure you get breakfast just the way you want it. The menu sports seven varieties of eggs Benedict. Not into hollandaise sauce? No problem. Skip down the menu to the loaded omelets. Try the cracked egg omelet. It has everything but an eggshell. Looking for a vegetarian option? Try the Greek omelet or the veggie, all packed with fresh ingredients. The apple fritters are a crowd favorite. Made with freshly chopped Granny Smith apples and then dipped in the special homemade batter, these are made to order and coated in cinnamon sugar before being whisked to your table. Lunch options include hot and cold sandwiches (including egg salad of course), and burgers. After your meal, you may need to cross Atlantic Avenue and take a long walk on the beach.

3280 S Atlantic Ave., Ste. D, Daytona Beach Shores, 386-788-6772
thecrackedeggdiner.com

TIP

If you are trying to find the Cracked Egg Diner, on the west side of Atlantic Avenue, keep your eyes peeled for the Eggulance, a bright yellow, repurposed ambulance, sporting the restaurant's logo, a chicken coming out of a "cracked egg."

8

SQUEEZE INTO VEGETARIAN CUISINE

AT KALE CAFE VEGAN KITCHEN

Kale Cafe Vegan Kitchen owners Camille Holder-Brown and Omar Brown operate their business with the twin goals of educating and serving their customers and the Daytona Beach community. They promote a vegetarian option without sacrificing flavor. After moving to Daytona Beach from New York state in 2011, the couple first opened their restaurant in 2013 as a not-for-profit organization named Midtown Eco Village before rebranding as Kale Cafe in 2014. The owners describe their food as a blend of Caribbean and soul foods, a nod to their Jamaican heritage. Their food pays tribute to Camille and Omar's mothers and grandmothers.

Kale Cafe avoids processed foods, instead opting for locally grown and organic foods whenever possible. All pastas are made with non-GMO wheat. The veggie burger patties are made in-house. The stars here are juices and smoothies. Available in three sizes and made right in front of you, these are a juice-lover's dream. Give the Berry Bliss smoothie a try.

110 N Beach St., 386-236-8593
kalecafejuicebar.com

After enjoying a hand-prepared meal crafted with the finest ingredients, you will want to take home a bottle or two of the homemade Judah's Salad Dressing and Marinade, named after the couple's youngest child.

9

RACE INTO
THE BRICKYARD LOUNGE

Most race fans equate the name Brickyard with the world-famous Indianapolis 500. NASCAR fans will remind them it's the Brickyard 400 that matters. The restaurant's name, however, comes from the building's brick exterior. No matter the naming origins, what matters at the Brickyard Lounge are the burgers. The half-pound burgers are packed with flavor, loaded with your choice of toppings, and served with fries. You will leave full.

Located in a unique, two-story A-frame building near Bethune-Cookman University, the Brickyard has been a Daytona Beach staple for more than 30 years. It's long been a favorite of NASCAR executives and drivers, and local residents and visitors keep coming back for the food, atmosphere, and the opportunity for a chance meeting with a favorite driver. New owners Jeromie and Annette Allan have given the restaurant a cosmetic update while keeping the original feel and flavor diners have come to expect. While burgers are the go-to, the Brickyard also offers an assortment of sandwiches, wings, and salads.

747 W International Speedway Blvd., 386-253-2270
brickyardlounge.com

BUY A BIB AND TRY THESE AMAZING BURGERS

Big Mike's Burgers and More

1112 W Canal St., New Smyrna Beach, 386-957-4975
facebook.com/p/Big-Mikes-Burgers-NSB-100093988809741

The Breakers Restaurant

518 Flager Ave., New Smyrna Beach, 386-428-2019
breakersnsb.com

Daytona Taproom

310 Seabreeze Blvd., 386-872-3298
facebook.com/p/Daytona-Taproom-100044190082852

Lost Lagoon Wings & Grill

2004 N Dixie Fwy., New Smyrna Beach
386-366-3360
facebook.com/p/Lost-Lagoon-Wings-Grill-100031641230879

Ocean Deck

127 S Ocean Ave., 386-253-5224
oceandeck.com

10

ENJOY THE RIVER VIEWS

AT AUNT CATFISH'S ON THE RIVER

Pull into the parking lot at Aunt Catfish's on the River on any Sunday morning and you are likely to see a line of hungry diners waiting for a table. Get there early or you'll be joining the wait. On Sundays, the all-you-can-eat buffet, available until 2 p.m., is your best choice. The carving station, featuring ham, roast beef, and turkey, is a favorite. Kick off your weekend with live music on the patio every Friday and Saturday evening while enjoying your favorite beverage from the full-service bar. For seafood lovers, Aunt Catfish's regular menu offers everything from salmon to alligator, and from lobster to catfish. Chicken, burgers, and a large kids' menu are available. Save room for the Boat Sinker Pie or the homemade key lime pie. Aunt Catfish's is a local dining legend, having served up the famous cinnamon rolls and other crowd-pleasing fare for more than 45 years.

4009 Halifax Dr., Port Orange, 386-767-4768
auntcatfishontheriver.com

TIP

Did you get caught in the wait for a table? Not to worry; take a walk on the pier and enjoy the views of the Halifax River. Are the kids getting anxious? There's a playground available to keep them occupied. These amenities will make the wait time fly by.

11

EXPERIENCE BEACH LIFE
AT HYDE PARK PRIME STEAKHOUSE

Hyde Prime Steakhouse is located in one of Daytona Beach's finest hotels, the Hilton Daytona Beach Oceanfront Resort, conveniently located across A1A from the Daytona Beach Ocean Center. Whether you dine indoors or outdoors on the casual dining terrace, you will enjoy views of the hard-packed beach, with waves from the Atlantic Ocean crashing in. During the summer, take in the weekend sounds of classic rock, soul, and more, coming from bands playing at the nearby Bandshell. If you are looking for a group setting, ask about reserving the private dining area which can accommodate parties of up to 60. Steaks take the checkered flag here, with offerings named after famous NASCAR drivers. If you want to go for the win, try the Denny Hamlin steak, a 38-ounce broiled tomahawk rib eye cooked with only salt, pepper, and steak seasoning. Once cooked and rested, it is topped with Cajun butter for your enjoyment.

100 N Atlantic Ave., 386-226-9844
hydeparkrestaurants.com/location/daytona-beach

TIP

If you want great steak but don't want to dine in, order your favorite meal online and schedule a pickup time convenient for you.

12

TRAVEL TO ITALY
AT THE GARLIC AND BLU BAR

Whether you dine indoors or take a seat at one of the many patio tables, the minute you arrive at the Garlic and Blu Bar, you will feel as if you have been transported to Old World Italy. Walk past the 800-degree wood-fired oven where many of the dishes on the menu are cooked. See the homemade bread coming out to servers ready to please their diners. Take in the daily specials, handwritten on sheets of uncooked lasagna noodles. Order wine, beer, or mixed drinks off the extensive alcohol list. Sit back and enjoy live music while your server crushes fresh garlic at your table to go with your bread. Try to save room for the tiramisu or seven-layer carrot cake. Featured on Guy Fieri's *Diners, Drive-Ins, and Dives*, the Garlic is more than dining—it's a total sensory experience.

556 E 3rd Ave., New Smyrna Beach, 386-424-6660
thegarlic.net

TIP

The Garlic does not take reservations. Seating is first come, first served. If you don't want to wait for a table, arrive near opening at 4 p.m. or after 8:30 p.m., when wait times are shorter.

13

CLIMB HIGH
AT NORWOOD'S EATERY & BAR

When Earl Norwood bought an old general store building in 1946 and turned it into Norwood's Seafood Restaurant, he could hardly have imagined that 80 years later the restaurant would be reaching to the sky with a treehouse bar in addition to the seafood favorites he served up. A longtime local favorite is the smoked fish dip made with smoked mahi-mahi. Beef is aged in-house a minimum of 40 days, and steaks are hand-cut. Fresh seafood, right off the boat, including grouper, tuna, salmon, and mahi-mahi, can be cooked your way—grilled, blackened, broiled, or fried. Among the hottest spots in New Smyrna Beach are seats in the Treehouse Bar. Enjoy dinner or just imbibe at the bar from the extensive selection of vodka, rum, scotch, rye, and bourbon. Order your favorite mixed drink and watch the sun set on another beautiful Florida day.

400 E 2nd Ave., New Smyrna Beach, 386-428-4621
norwoods.com

TIP

If you are planning a special event, give Norwood's a call and reserve the Garden Patio, the Coquina Room, or the Roots Patio & Bar. With amazing views and unparalleled service, it will be an event you and your guests will never forget.

14

SATISFY YOUR SWEET TOOTH
AT TREATS & SWEETS CAKERY

After earning employee of the year while still a teen working at Aunt Catfish's on the River, Treats & Sweets Cakery owner Justine Knight discovered her passion while taking a cake-decorating course at a local store. She went on to graduate from Daytona State College, and in 2013 she opened her business. Now, more than a decade later, Knight and her business are highly regarded, regularly working with high-profile clients such as the NASCAR Foundation, Michael Jordan, and NASCAR driver Rusty Wallace. Knight has not forgotten her roots, however. Her storefront offers delicious cakes, cookies, cupcakes, and more for walk-in clients. Special orders and custom-designed sweets are a specialty. For a wedding cake that every guest will remember, schedule a tasting and design consultation before going anywhere else.

2002 S Ridgewood Ave., South Daytona, 386-383-8256
yourcakery.com

TIP

Wednesdays are special at Treats & Sweets Cakery, as in-store cupcake purchases are buy-two-get-one-free. Gluten- and dairy-free options are available. Your sweet tooth will be working overtime.

FEED YOUR SUGAR CRAVINGS AT THESE BAKERIES

Buttercup Bakery

197 E Church St., DeLand, 386-736-4043
instagram.com/buttercupdeland

Flagler Tea Company

208 S Central Ave., Ste. B, Flagler Beach, 386-631-3962
flaglertea.com

Kneading More Sweets

175 S Nova Rd., Ste. 7, Ormond Beach, 386-673-7989
kneadingmoresweets.com

The French Bakery & Pastry Shop

359 W Granada Blvd., Ormond Beach, 386-672-5594
facebook.com/thefrenchbakeryfl

Mon Délice French Bakery

557 E 3rd Ave., New Smyrna Beach, 386-427-6555
mondelicebakery.com

Rosie's Italian Bakery & Café

232 Bay St., 386-236-8995
facebook.com/RosiesItalianBakeryCafe

15

EVERYONE'S A LITTLE IRISH

AT McK'S TAVERN & BREWERY

If you can't visit Ireland, McK's Tavern downtown will get you close with its authentic feel. The food and drink options are numerous and varied. From Irish classics such as bangers and mash and shepherd's pie to the classic fish and chips, you will find it on the menu. A wide range of burgers, sandwiches, and salads are also available, as are vegetarian options. What's an Irish pub without beer? McK's serves up a large assortment of locally brewed favorites along with a limited number of more widely distributed brands. Can you get a properly poured Guinness? Of course—it's an Irish pub! With more than 125 beers on tap, bottled, canned, and in growlers, there's something for every beer lover. Try the McK's Connors Irish Red, their flagship beer. Be sure to get there early to hear the best in local live music.

218 S Beach St., 386-238-3321
mckstavernandbrewery.com

16

SPEED ON IN
TO RACING'S NORTH TURN

Imagine sitting right where the earliest Daytona Beach NASCAR races were held. A visit to Racing's North Turn allows you to do just that. You'll be sitting at the north turn, where the best drivers of the day exited the hard-packed sands along the Atlantic Ocean and began the drive south, along the paved roadway. Be sure to see the historic marker outside the restaurant commemorating the location. Inside, you will be treated to a free racing museum including cars, uniforms, photos, and signed memorabilia. Dine outside on the large patio, or maybe sit at the bar while listening to the waves while watching beachgoers stroll the sands. Make plans to be there in February and attend the Legends Beach Parade to see the old cars back on the beach. Even though they are not racing, these race cars of yesterday are a must-see for any NASCAR fan.

4511 S Atlantic Ave., Ponce Inlet, 386-322-3258
northturnemail.wixsite.com/my-site-1

TIP

Visit for lunch at noon on a Friday to catch the recording of the *Legends of Racing* radio show. You never know who will be a guest.

17

BRING OUT YOUR INNER LUMBERJACK
AT IRON AXE BAR & GRILL

One of the latest entertainment trends is axe throwing, and Daytona Beach has a great location to participate. Yes, you are throwing real axes at real wooden targets. What separates Iron Axe is the use of digital targets and interactive games as part of the experience. Are you new to axe throwing? Not to worry; ask your server for tips (and be sure to leave them a tip as well). Dining options aren't just regular bar food. Ingredients are sourced locally when possible. Try everything from burgers and mouthwatering steaks to pastas and salads. Daily specials are offered. Make Iron Axe Bar & Grill your home away from home for all your sporting favorites. With 22 screens and all the major packages and pay-per-views, you won't miss a minute of the action. Go for the food even if you don't want to throw an axe.

2842 S Ridgewood Ave., South Daytona, 386-238-9170
ironaxebar.com

TIP

The six axe-throwing lanes fill up fast, and it is recommended to book online ahead of time. Walk-ins are taken only if space is available. Online reservations are for one hour. Walk-ins are allowed only a half hour of lane time depending upon availability. And don't forget close-toed shoes, a requirement for participating.

18

EAT LIKE A BOSS AT CORLEONE'S FAMOUS NEW YORK PIZZA & GYROS

Pizza comes in all varieties. It may be Detroit, Chicago, Greek, California, or some other style. If it's New York–style pizza you're after, Daytona Beach has an excellent spot to try: Corleone's Famous New York Pizza & Gyros. The name brings to mind *The Godfather* and Marlon Brando. The self-proclaimed Pizza Don, Corleone's owner Alex Fotiadis, grew up in his family's pizza restaurants. Since breaking out on his own in 2002, he has been using only imported San Marzano tomatoes for his sauce and the highest quality flour for his dough, which is allowed to mature for several days. The pizzas are topped with cheeses sourced directly from a Wisconsin farm. You will never go wrong with the large pepperoni. The pizzas are so good, you'll swear you are in New York City. *Deliziosa*!

505 White St., 386-333-9996
corleonesny.com

FIND A DELICIOUS, HOT PIZZA, WHETHER DINE IN, DELIVERY, OR TAKE OUT

Alberto's Pizzeria

1501 S Ridgewood Ave.
Edgewater, 386-424-1514
albertositalianrestaurant.com/home

Baci Pizzeria Ristorante

830 N Dixie Fwy.
New Smyrna Beach
386-410-5801
bacipizzaristorante.com

Bronx House Pizza

1290 W Granada Blvd.
#200, Ormond Beach
386-888-6699
bronxhousepizza.com/ormond/index.php

Genovese's Italian Cafe

Multiple locations

Luigi's Pizza and Ristorante

3824 Clyde Morris Blvd.
Port Orange
386-761-6633
luigisclydemorris.com

Pagano's Pizzeria

1945 Ridgewood Ave.
South Dayona
386-767-3635
paganospizzerias.com

Panheads Pizzeria

113 S Orange Ave.
New Smyrna Beach
386-428-8738
panheadspizzeria.com

Pete's Pizza

1441 S Nova Rd.
386-253-3707
petespizzadaytona.com

Touch of Italy

4198 S Atlantic Ave.
New Smyrna Beach
386-423-8956
italianrestaurantnewsmyrnabeach.com

19

WATCH THE SUNSET

AT OUR DECK DOWN UNDER

Whether you are a boater or a landlubber, nobody can resist the river views provided at Our Deck Down Under. Tired after a day on the river? Tie your boat up on the Deck's convenient dock before ordering a drink and food at the counter. A server will bring it to your table. This local landmark has been serving up delicious food from "down under" the Dunlawton Bridge for more than 20 years. It's located on the Intracoastal Waterway, a stone's throw from the Atlantic Ocean, and fresh seafood is the order of the day, whether fried, grilled, or blackened. Not a seafood fan? There are plenty of fresh salads and sandwiches to choose from. Sit back, relax, and enjoy the river views. You may be lucky and see dolphins, manatees, turtles, and all varieties of birds. This is what people imagine when they dream of Florida.

78 Dunlawton Ave., Port Orange, 386-767-1881
ourdeckdownunder.com

RELIVE THE LIFE OF A LOCAL LEGEND AT CARIBBEAN JACK'S

When John "Jack" Gilbert saw an opportunity to profit from illicit booze brought to the states from the Caribbean during the Prohibition years, he took advantage. Gilbert supplied spirits up and down the east coast of Florida before retiring to the life of restaurant owner in Daytona Beach. Today, Caribbean Jack's, located on the Halifax River in the Loggerhead Marina, honors the legacy of the man who is claimed to have stated "time flies when you're having rum" with a menu any Prohibition-era rumrunner would have loved. Seafood, ribs, chicken, and pastas pack the menu. The fish Reuben, made with haddock, melted Swiss cheese, and a rémoulade on rye, is a sandwich diners come back for time and time again. Save room for a piece of house-made key lime pie or the signature bananas Foster, made with a rum Jack Gilbert would have been proud to sell. They don't accept reservations, so get there early and enjoy live musical entertainment every night beginning at 5 p.m.

721 Ballough Rd., 386-523-3000 (also 844-655-3000)
caribbeanjacks.com

21

VISIT THAILAND
AT ZEN BISTRO

From humble beginnings nearly two decades ago with a restaurant that could seat only 30 patrons, Zen Bistro quickly developed a loyal following, necessitating a larger footprint. Today, to visit Zen Bistro is to be taken to a different world. Step through the gate and walk under the traditional arch while the sound of wind chimes and softly running water help take you away from the daily grind of your nine-to-five. Whether you choose to dine on the bamboo-surrounded patio with the warmth of a firepit for company, or inside where you will delight at the handwoven silks adorning the walls, the owners and staff at Zen Bistro want to make this your private oasis. You will find all your favorites on the menu, made with the finest ingredients. Soups, curries, noodles, and more are available. Everything is made from scratch at your preferred heat levels, so you'll be planning your return visit before you leave.

223 Magnolia Ave., 386-248-0453
zenbistrodaytona.com

22

DIVE DEEP INTO THE FRESHEST SEAFOOD
AT HULL'S SEAFOOD

By age 20, Jimmy Hull was already a certified boat captain and running both commercial and charter fishing boats out of Ponce Inlet, where he would unload the day's catch, selling to local fish markets. In 1981, Hull opened his own retail seafood market, and in 2005, he expanded further by offering take-out seafood from a small kitchen. This success prompted further expansion, and today Hull's Seafood offers indoor and outdoor seating along with fresh, take-home seafood for home cooking.

Dine in-house for the freshest seafood you will find. With offerings from crab cakes and fish chowder to line-caught tuna, mahi-mahi, and the best fried grouper sandwich available, Hull's is a seafood lover's paradise. If your eyes aren't bigger than your stomach, try the blueberry hush puppies. Can't make it to the restaurant? For a small charge, Hull's delivers their fresh fish for you to cook at home.

111 W Granada Blvd., Ormond Beach, 386-673-8888
bestseafoodinfl.com

23

RELIVE SUMMERS OF YOUR YOUTH

AT BAY STREET DAWGS

Seeking to revive that "small town feeling" in his newly adopted town of Daytona Beach, owner and professionally trained chef Gary Tolla brings back those vibes of yesteryear, serving up delicious hot dogs and hamburgers like you enjoyed at family cookouts, only elevated. Served on a split top bun, these beef dawgs are a delicacy plain. Tolla rachets up the flavor with the Pit Road Dawg, covered in barbecue sauce, bacon, grilled onions, and cheddar cheese sauce. Or maybe the Mario Dawg, with hot relish, chili, cheese sauce, and raw onions is your speed. If you aren't worried about making a mess, the Reuben Dawg, with sauerkraut, Swiss cheese, and Thousand Island dressing is for you. There's even a Bay Street Vegan Dawg that you can customize. Finish your meal with the massive chili cheese fries or the onion petals. Order ahead and pick up at your convenience. Dawgs have never tasted so good.

108 Bay St., 386-492-7589
baystreetdawgs.weebly.com

24

ENJOY THE BEST IN SOUTHERN FOOD
AT HILL'S CHICKEN & WAFFLES

From fried pork chops and smoked turkey to a classic shrimp and grits or oxtail, it's food your grandmother would have been proud to serve. Wanting something a bit lighter? Try the chicken or shrimp salad. The shrimp po boy with all the toppings is a crowd pleaser. The star, of course, is the chicken and waffles combo. Choose from breast, drumstick, wings, or thighs, or order family style and try them all. Then move to your waffle options. I suggest keeping it basic for the first visit with a buttermilk waffle that has a good hint of vanilla in the batter. Want something a bit out of the ordinary? Try the Fruity Pebbles, Oreo, or maybe the red velvet waffle.

2120 S Ridgewood Ave., Ste. 8, Edgewater, 689-239-2481
facebook.com/Hills.Chicken.and.Waffles

25

QUENCH YOUR CAFFEINE ADDICTION

AT COPPERLINE COFFEE

Copperline Coffee, which takes its name from the James Taylor song, was founded in order to cultivate a space that is not just a coffee house but also a community hub. Today, no matter which of the Copperline shops you step into, you will see friends gathering, remote workers at work, students studying, and authors hunched over their manuscripts. All these members of the Copperline community are achieving their daily goals over a cup of something delicious. The coffee may be drip, French Press, or pour-over. It might be an espresso, a latte, or a cappuccino. Some will even be sipping a freshly brewed Moroccan green tea. If you want something a bit more substantial, the cinnamon sugar biscuit with a vanilla cinnamon glaze is highly recommended. Pair it with your favorite cup of joe, and all your problems will seem to melt away.

5521 S Williamson Blvd., #420, Port Orange, 386-310-7139
118 S Beach St., Daytona Beach, 386-265-4731
copperlinecoffee.com

FIND YOUR MORNING CAFFEINE PICK-ME-UP

Beach Bros Coffee Company

140 S Atlantic Ave., Daytona Beach
3738 Halifax Dr., Port Orange
386-232-9089
beachbroscoffee.com
facebook.com/people/Beach-Bros-Coffee-Port-Orange/61582262632274

Boston Coffee House

Multiple locations, 386-738-2326
facebook.com/BostonCoffeehouseDeLand

Gold Leaf Coffee

17 W Granada Blvd., Ormond Beach, 386-301-5652
goldleafcoffee.com

Island Roasters Coffee Company

398 N Causeway, New Smyrna Beach, 386-847-2920
islandroasterscoffeecompany.com

King's Koffee

Pelican Plaza, 2349 S Ridgewood Ave., Edgewater
406-235-0401
facebook.com/people/Kings-Koffee/61556704775429

Serra Doce

214 S Beach St., 386-256-5323
serradocedaytona.com

Trilogy Coffee Cafe

136 W Georgia Ave., DeLand, 386-624-6057
trilogycoffee.com/trilogy-coffee-cafe

Boot Hill Saloon

MUSIC AND ENTERTAINMENT

KNOW WHEN TO HOLD'EM
AT DAYTONA BEACH RACING & CARD CLUB

The current incarnation of what is often called the Daytona Poker Room opened in 2008 after having been located adjacent to Daytona International Speedway when greyhound racing was the primary attraction. Today greyhound racing has been banned in the state of Florida, and the business has evolved into a thriving card club. Try your hand at one of the low buy-in poker games. Think you are an expert player? Not to worry—there are monthly high-dollar tournaments. Whether you play five card stud, pineapple, Omaha, Texas Hold'em, or other poker variants, there's a table and dealer waiting for you. Complimentary nonalcoholic drinks are available for players.

Not a card player? Head over to the personal betting screens and wager on simulcast horse and greyhound races, or jai alai.

960 S Williamson Blvd., 386-252-6484
www.daytonabeachpoker.com

TIP

Are you on the west side of the county? Try Orange City Racing & Card Club.

822–4 Saxon Blvd., Orange City, 386-252-6484
orangecitypoker.com

27

CRUISE THE INTRACOASTAL

ON THE *LADY DOLPHIN OF DAYTONA*

Florida's Intracoastal Waterway offers amazing views. An hour and a half cruise on the *Lady Dolphin of Daytona* provides the opportunity to see dolphins, manatees, sea turtles, birds of all species, and more. Just sit back and enjoy the gentle river breezes while taking in all the natural beauty the Halifax River has to offer. Did I mention that dinner is included? Choose from delicious shrimp scampi, baked ham, oven-roasted turkey, or prime rib. For vegetarians there are pasta options available. Dessert and unlimited soft drinks come with the meal. A cash bar is available if you prefer something a bit harder. Arrive early for your preferred seat location. The enclosed lower level is air conditioned while the upper level is open to the elements. Cruises depart multiple times per day, so make reservations for a time that is convenient for you.

125 Basin St., Ste. 140, 386-402-1353
dineandcruise.com

TIP

While this may seem like a chance to dress up for an exciting date, the crew of the *Lady Dolphin* recommend dressing for comfort, especially when it comes to footwear. Floors can become slippery, and shoes not suitable for wet surfaces are discouraged.

SWING YOUR HIPS LIKE ELVIS AT THE PEABODY AUDITORIUM

Did you know a very young Elvis Presley played in Daytona Beach at the Peabody Auditorium, not just once but several times? It's true. Named for Daytona Beach businessman Simon J. Peabody, the modern version of the Peabody Auditorium was dedicated in 1949. The Peabody has seen a who's who in the music and theater world pass through its doors. Today the Peabody seats around 2,500 and regularly hosts productions from Broadway and rock, pop, and country musical acts popular then and now. Comedians and tribute acts to the biggest stars also take the historic stage, playing to large crowds nightly. If classical music or opera is more your speed, the Daytona Beach Symphony Society occasionally hosts touring orchestras here. If you enjoy ballet, the annual performance of the *Nutcracker* by Volusia Civic Ballet is a perfect December evening.

600 Auditorium Blvd., 386-671-3462
peabodyauditorium.org

TIP

Directly across Auditorium Boulevard is the Daytona Beach Ocean Center. The Ocean Center hosts a wide variety of concerts, sporting events, conventions, graduations, and more. Be sure to see the incredible permanent art collection on display throughout.

ROCK THE NIGHT AWAY
AT BEACHSIDE TAVERN

Come as you are, whether off the beach or ready for a night on the town, and get ready to party every night of the week as Beachside Tavern brings you the best in original music, tribute bands, cover bands, live comedy, and watch parties. Whether you like hard rock, ska, acoustic, or country, it's on the calendar. It doesn't matter if you want to stop in for lunch or if you're a night owl who parties until early in the morning, this is your spot. Come hungry and thirsty and try the amazing bar foods such as burgers, wings, and pizza while enjoying your favorite beverage from the well-stocked bar. Shoot a few games of pool or catch all the sports action on the large-screen televisions. Don't miss New Smyrna's "Best Original Live Music Venue," conveniently located just a short drive from the beach and the action on Flagler Avenue.

690 E 3rd Ave., New Smyrna Beach, 386-424-8282
beachsidetavern.com

TAKE THE STAGE
AT DAYTONA PLAYHOUSE

Since 1946, the volunteer-operated Daytona Playhouse has provided local thespians of all ages and experience levels the opportunity to stretch their creative wings on stage. The 1955 theater building has undergone considerable renovations in the last decade, adding more than 2,000 square feet, enhancing their ADA qualifications and upgrading air conditioning and heating. Seating 260 patrons, Daytona Playhouse is an intimate yet upgraded venue where it is said there are no bad sight lines. Today, a year-round season featuring dramas, musicals, and comedies keeps theater-goers returning. Every December, Daytona Playhouse presents a holiday-themed performance that is one of the most sought-after tickets in town.

The Playhouse's Young Actors Company provides ample opportunities for selected students aged 11 to 19 to gain valuable experience, whether on stage or in production roles. This free training program culminates each summer with live community theater productions.

100 Jessamine Blvd., 386-255-2431
daytonaplayhouse.org

31

CONNECT THE DOTS
AT DAYTONA ESCAPE ROOM EXPERIENCE

Do you have what it takes to solve some of Daytona Beach's trickiest puzzles? The Daytona Escape Room Experience offers groups of all sizes the opportunity to match wits with nearly a dozen rooms and challenges. From bank heists to a pirate ship on the high seas to a bomb set to explode, you and your team have one hour to solve the puzzles and escape.

All Daytona Escape Room Experience visits must be booked online in advance. Your visit will be private, and you will not be sharing an escape room with other groups. These rooms are perfect for team-building exercises, family fun, or an exciting night out for you and your friends. Games are rated by difficulty, so you are able to cater your visit to your experience level. Bring your critical thinking and observation skills and beat the clock. You have one hour to escape!

679 Beville Rd., South Daytona, 386-689-2124
daytonaescaperoom.com

32

LAUNCH INTO THE SKY
ON THE DAYTONA BEACH SLINGSHOT

Adrenaline junkies, this one is for you. Take your choice of the Daytona Slingshot or the Vomatron, and be prepared for an experience unlike any you have had. In less than two seconds, the slingshot will launch you 360 feet in the air at speeds up to 100 miles per hour. And just when you think it's done, you are racing skyward again. The Vomatron is similar to astronaut training methods. You'll be rocketed at speeds reaching 70 miles per hour in a spinning capsule, reaching forces of up to 5 g as the 165-foot arm circulates, only to reverse direction, further spinning and disorienting you. Afraid your friends won't believe that you did it? Buy the video package and prove it. Once back on firm ground you will want to stagger over to Screamer's Bar for a soft drink or maybe something a bit stronger. This isn't for the faint of heart.

25 S Atlantic Ave., 386-944-9861
slingshotdaytonabeach.com

TIP

For a unique experience, ride the Slingshot after dark and see Daytona Beach lit up from high above. Pay attention to the rapidly changing weather, however. If there's lighting around, you won't be able to ride.

GET DRESSED UP FOR A NIGHT

WITH THE DAYTONA BEACH SYMPHONY SOCIETY

Founded in 1952, the Daytona Beach Symphony Society has been presenting the finest classical music and opera to the Volusia County area for more than 70 years. No longer do residents have to travel to New York or other distant locales to attend concerts from organizations such as the Czech National Philharmonic Orchestra, the Kyiv Virtuosi Symphony Orchestra, the Russian National Orchestra, and many more. So put on your finest dress or suit, make dinner reservations at a favorite restaurant, and have a date night you won't forget. The Society does not have its own venue, and most of their events take place at the News-Journal Center at Daytona State College or the Peabody Auditorium.

The Symphony Society's Youth Experiencing Symphony (YES!) Program targets at-risk youth and since 1995 has introduced more than 60,000 students in public, private, and home schools to classical music.

News-Journal Center Box Office
221 N Beach St., 386-226-1888
dbss.org

Become a season subscriber and never miss a show. You can reserve your preferred seats at the best prices by subscribing. Subscriptions are available at several price points, making this a great option for classical music enthusiasts.

34

PEDAL YOUR CARES AWAY
WITH PADDLE PUB DAYTONA BEACH

Take a ride on the ultimate Daytona Beach party boat! Paddle Pub offers seating for up to 20 people on their pedal-powered pontoon boat. Dress comfortably and get ready for a two-hour cruise along the Halifax River. This is a nonsmoking boat and operates rain or shine as long as the river conditions allow. The boat comes equipped with coolers and a sound system, so bring your own food and drinks (but none of the really hard stuff or glass bottles, please), along with your favorite music, and get ready to party like you can only do in Daytona Beach. Because of the nature of these cruises, only those ages 18 and up are allowed during the public cruises.

Are you looking for the perfect bachelor or bachelorette party option? Maybe you want an opportunity for your work team to bond a bit more. Book a private tour and reserve the full boat. All ages are welcome on private cruises.

Halifax Harbor Marina
450 Basin St., 386-478-9207
paddlepub.com/daytonabeach

TIP

Don't feel up to pedaling while partying? No problem—the boat comes equipped with an engine and a Coast Guard–certified captain to make sure your cruise is not only memorable but safe.

35

SLIP AND SLIDE
AT DAYTONA LAGOON

There's no need to go to Orlando for water park, go-karting, and laser tag fun. Just head beachside and visit Daytona Lagoon. For the adventurous, climb to the top of Kraken's Revenge and rocket down the 50-foot drop. Or maybe the Pelican's Drift Lazy River is more your (slow) speed. Float around the park, taking in everything there is to see with none of the adrenaline rush of the high-speed rides. Dry off and race go-karts, or bump and spin while crashing through the bumper cars. Try your hand at the challenging mini-golf course, try to make it to the top of the rock wall, take target practice at laser tag, or play one of the more than 70 games in the Mega Arcade. For the young, or young at heart, Daytona Lagoon is a must-visit family fun attraction.

601 Earl St., 386-254-5020
daytonalagoon.com

TIP

Your best parking option is the County of Volusia–owned parking garage, located adjacent to the park. On hot days you'll appreciate coming back to a cool car. Elevators are available should you have difficulty with stairs. Be sure to have your parking ticket validated at the Daytona Lagoon admission desk to receive a discounted garage rate.

RELIEVE YOUR STRESS
AT RAGE ROOM DAYTONA BEACH

Have you had one of those days when it seemed that nothing went right? You probably caught every red light on the way to work. Three emergencies happened, and all of them needed your attention. The phone wouldn't stop ringing, and your boss just had to meet with you. Well, take out that frustration by booking your visit to Rage Room Daytona Beach. The Rage Room can accommodate from one to eight visitors. You choose the amount of time and number of items included at the time of booking. Get ready to swing hammers, baseball bats, and golf clubs. Take out your stress on glassware, ceramics, stereo equipment, televisions, printers (who hasn't wanted to hit a printer with a hammer?), furniture, and more. Bring your own items to add to the assortment or donate them for future users. You will leave exhausted but relieved. Therapy never felt so good.

639 N Ridgewood Ave., 386-309-2225
rageroomdaytona.com

TIP

First responders, military, healthcare workers, teachers, and linemen receive 10 percent off online bookings. Be sure to bring your ID at check-in.

PAY TRIBUTE TO YOUR FAVORITES

AT THE DAYTONA BEACH BANDSHELL

Dating to the years of the Franklin D. Roosevelt administration, the Daytona Beach Bandshell was one of the many successful local projects spearheaded by the Works Progress Administration. Since opening in July 1937, with a construction cost of around $265,000, the venue has served as home for a local symphony and *MTV Spring Break*, and it has hosted presidential campaign rallies. Today it offers regular concerts and fireworks shows. The Friends of the Bandshell, a nonprofit group founded in 1996, presents the annual Star-Spangled Summer Concerts series of Saturday evening concerts. An incredible fireworks performance over the ocean concludes each concert. In 1999, the coquina facility, which seats up to 3,500 persons, was added to the National Register of Historic Places as part of the Daytona Beach Oceanfront Bandshell and Ocean Front Park Complex.

70 Boardwalk, 386-671-3462
daytonabandshell.com

TIP

While visiting the Bandshell, don't miss the Coquina Clock Tower and fountain, located just to the south. The 55-foot-high clock tower has the letters D-A-Y-T-O-N-A-B-E-A-C-H instead of numerals on its face, a design as unique as Daytona Beach itself.

SADDLE UP TO THE BAR
AT THE BOOT HILL SALOON

If you ask locals to name a single biker bar in Daytona Beach, they will probably name the Boot Hill Saloon. It's easy to understand why. The name could not be more appropriate. Directly across Main Street is Pinewood Cemetery, one of the oldest and most historically significant cemeteries in Daytona Beach. Thus, the Saloon slogan, "Come On In, Grab a Seat, You're Better Off Here Than Across the Street." You don't have to live the biker lifestyle to enjoy the Boot Hill, however. Stepping inside, you will find the walls covered with all types of items left by patrons, from clothing to business cards and everything in between, including plenty of graffiti. While you may find yourself seated next to a legitimate biker gang member, you may just as easily be next to a banker, a student, or a celebrity who is in town. Visit for friends, cold beer, and great music, and don't forget to leave with a Boot Hill Saloon T-shirt to commemorate your visit.

310 E Main St., 386-258-9506
boothillsaloon.com

PUT YOUR KICKSTAND DOWN AT YOUR FAVORITE BIKER BAR

Dirty Harry's Pub & Package

705 Main St., 386-259-6000
dirtyharrysdaytonabeach.com

Ed Walden's Bar

745 S Beach St., 386-258-3935
facebook.com/EdWaldens

Froggy's Saloon

800 Main St., 386-253-0330
thefroggyssaloon.com

Iron Horse Saloon

1068 US Rte. 1, Ormond Beach, 386-677-1550
ironhorsesaloon.com

The Last Resort Bar

5812 S Ridgewood Ave., Port Orange, 386-761-5147
facebook.com/Lastresortbar

Sopotnik's Cabbage Patch Bar

549 Tomoka Farms Rd., New Smyrna Beach
386-427-8969
facebook.com/SopotnicksCabbagePatchBar

Sorry Charlie's Corner

3705 FL–44, New Smyrna Beach, 386-428-4858
sorrycharliescornerbar.com

HOBNOB LIKE A MOVIE STAR AT CINEMATIQUE OF DAYTONA

For 35 years, Cinematique of Daytona has been Volusia County's only independent, nonprofit, art house cinema. In 2010, Cinematique found its permanent home, a quaint 70-seat theater showing films on a 25-foot screen. Today, Cinematique provides a unique opportunity for theater-goers to see first-run, art house, Academy Award–quality films that they might otherwise have had to drive to Orlando, Tampa, or Jacksonville to view. Most presentations, including foreign language films, contain subtitles, making them accessible to all viewers. Not just a cinema, Cinematique also features local and touring comedians weekly, improv shows, live music, and more. Check their online schedule to see what's showing. Hungry? Cinematique provides a limited range of food and drink options that will satisfy your cravings, and there are also plenty of locally owned restaurants along Beach Street if you are looking for a full meal. With tickets prices comparable to the standard box office, make Cinematique a stop on your Daytona Beach bucket list.

242 S Beach St., 386-252-3118
cinematique.org

40

PLAY ARCADE GAMES ALL DAY
AT GAME TIME

Relive those days of youth when you used to pop quarters into your favorite arcade game in the Mega Arcade at Game Time. Here you will find everything from arcade classics such as *Pong* to updated games including *Pac-Man Battle Royale*, a four-person race to eat the most pellets, and maybe even your competitors. Find ride simulators, games of skill, and games of chance, and warm up your arm for the most competitive game of air hockey you have ever played. Have you been bowling recently? Game Time has multiple lanes and playing options. With more than 100 games available, there's something for everyone to enjoy. All this fun is bound to make you hungry, so stop in at the on-site sports bar for pizza, burgers, salads, and more. Adult beverages are available, and you won't miss any of the live sports action with more than 60 large-screen, high-definition televisions.

250 Daytona Blvd., 386-944-5495
gametimeplayers.com/home-daytona

TIP

There's no need to bring quarters or worry about the bill changer not taking your dollar bills. Buy your reloadable all-access card and play any game you wish.

FACE YOUR FEARS
AT THE REPTILE DISCOVERY CENTER

Readers, you can admit it. Many of you have a fear of snakes. It's nothing to be ashamed of. If you want to get over that fear, a visit to the Reptile Discovery Center may be just what you need. Outside on the nature trail you will see many species of reptiles, including alligators, lizards, tortoises, and more, all enclosed for your safety and theirs. It's inside where the real magic happens, however. Indoor exhibits include rattlesnakes, cobras, mambas, and many other venomous snakes. See a rare white rattlesnake and a taipan. Native to Australia and New Guinea, taipans are among the world's most venomous snakes. The center is home to Medtoxin Venom Laboratories, a commercial venom production facility that provides manufacturers snake venom for producing lifesaving antivenom. Researchers are using snake venom in cancer research, immunological and transplant research, diabetes research, and other areas.

2710 Big John Dr., DeLand, 386-740-9143
reptilediscoverycenter.com

TIP

Don't miss the live venom extraction program, which is held several times each week. Still a bit squeamish at the idea of large, poisonous snakes? Not to worry, this dangerous process occurs behind safety glass and is conducted by trained professionals. Venom extraction days and times can be found on the website.

42

HAVE A CIGAR; YOU'RE GONNA GO FAR

AT JOE'S CIGAR ROOM

Since 2022, Joe's Cigar Room has offered visitors and residents the finest quality cigars from a wide range of makers. Step into the dark wooded rooms and take a load off your feet in the overstuffed, leather-upholstered chairs. Joe's has taken care of everything you'll need. Humidors are filled with the finest cigars and plenty of cigar accessories available for purchase. The air ventilation system keeps the rooms from becoming smoke-filled and uncomfortable. Enjoy a cold beverage, including beer and wine. Make new friends over a competitive game of backgammon, dominos, or cards, or maybe just relax and watch one of the giant screen televisions. Once you've had your fill inside, step out onto the large, screened-in patio area that will keep the mosquitoes away. Open late on Friday and Saturday evenings, Joe's will keep you coming back for great friends and great cigars.

400 S Myrtle Ave., New Smyrna Beach, 386-402-8871
joescigarnsb.com

TIP

Don't have your own humidor? Take advantage of the Cigar Humidor Locker program at Joe's. Buy your cigars and store them on-site until you are ready to smoke them. If you are a regular customer, inquire about discounts on box purchases.

DISCOVER THE UNEXPECTED

AT DAYTONA AQUARIUM AND RAINFOREST ADVENTURE

When you walk through the front entrance, which is painted like an undersea adventure, be prepared to be taken to a new world. Take a self-guided tour of Frog Swamp and Lizard Lair before coming close to some of nature's fiercest creatures at Gator Alley and Shark Reef. Witness fish with vibrant colors that can be found only in the deepest ocean areas. Head over to the Touch Pool and touch a stingray while watching them interact with humans and each other. Octopuses are masters of disguise. Will you be able to find them? Don't miss the Rainforest Adventure portion of the attraction, where visitors are able to witness exotic birds such as the toucan, the loveable sloth, tamarins, Asian small-claw otters, and more in an authentic environment. For the techie in the family, seek out the seven virtual reality experiences. You might just get bumped by a shark. Are you looking for a place to hold a birthday party or other special events? Look no further than the party rooms. Daytona Aquarium and Rainforest Adventure offers fun for all ages.

1008 W International Speedway Blvd., 386-241-3144
daytonaaquariumandrainforest.com

TIP

Don't confuse Daytona Aquarium and Rainforest Adventure with Cichlid Express, which is also known locally as Daytona Aquarium. Both are located on International Speedway Boulevard. Cichlid Express is a popular retailer of live freshwater fish for home aquariums, having been in business more than 30 years.

Dale Earnhardt
at Daytona International Speedway

SPORTS AND RECREATION

DIP YOUR TOES IN THE ATLANTIC

AT THE WORLD'S MOST FAMOUS BEACH

Volusia County beaches were home to what were called "beach races" for many years. These races initially consisted of time trials, where many world records were set during low tide and many lives were lost on the dangerous sands. In the early days of NASCAR, stock cars raced a beach and road combination track in Ponce Inlet that is commemorated at Racing's North Turn restaurant.

Once you take a drive or walk on the wide, hard-packed sands of Daytona Beach, you will understand why it is called the World's Most Famous Beach. With 47 miles of shoreline, Volusia County features beaches for driving, non-vehicular traffic, and sections allowing dogs. Whether you want to sunbathe, surf, swim, fish, exercise, or just go for a cruise, Daytona Beach is ready for you. Don't forget your sunscreen!

County of Volusia Beach Safety
386-239-7873
volusia.org/services/public-protection/beach-safety

TIP

For out-of-county drivers and non-registered county residents, there are daily fees. See the website and click the "driving, parking, and passes" tab for details.

RELIVE CIVIL RIGHTS HISTORY
AT JACKIE ROBINSON BALLPARK

When Jackie Robinson took the field at City Island Ballpark in Daytona Beach on March 17, 1946, he made history as the first African American player in modern baseball when his minor-league team, the Montreal Royals, took on the Brooklyn Dodgers. While Robinson was allowed to play, fans were segregated. He was not allowed to stay in the team hotel, instead rooming with local families. Today, the ballpark serves as a museum to Robinson's legacy and home to the Cincinnati Reds' minor-league team, the Daytona Tortugas. Tickets are available at family-friendly prices. Kids run the bases after every Sunday home game and Wednesdays are called Belly Buster Wednesdays, so come hungry!

The stadium is on the National Register of Historic Places and is a National Commemorative Site.

110 E Orange Ave., 386-257-3172
milb.com/daytona

TIP

Do not miss the many historic markers dedicated to Jackie Robinson throughout the stadium. Take a photo with the Jackie Robinson sculpture, located outside the bleachers on the right-field side of the ballpark.

46

DISCOVER WHY MANATEES LOVE BLUE SPRING STATE PARK

Every winter, hundreds of slow-moving, cold-averse manatees congregate in the 72-degree waters of Blue Spring. Here, these gentle giants are treated like royalty. Visitors by the thousands flock to Orange City for the opportunity to see these endangered mammals for themselves. Blue Spring isn't all manatees, however. A walk along the spring run, or the four-and-a-half-mile Pine Island Trail, may yield sightings of alligators, fish, ospreys, eagles, and more. For the more adventurous, you can rent kayaks and canoes and head out into the St. Johns River. If you would rather someone else be at the helm, enjoy a two-hour river cruise with park partner Blue Spring Adventures. The Thursby House is an 1872 home that served as a hub for steamboat passengers and will be a delight for the history lover in your group. Blue Spring offers an array of amenities including 51 pet-friendly campsites, six cabins, snorkeling, a limited scuba diving area, fishing, and a playground for the kids.

2100 W French Ave., Orange City, 386-775-3663
floridastateparks.org/parks-and-trails/blue-spring-state-park

TIP

On cold winter mornings, when manatee activity is at its highest, the park frequently reaches capacity and will close temporarily to allow for parking to open and a less congested park for visitors. These temporary closures apply to vehicles, bicyclists, and pedestrians. If you don't want to get on the bad side of locals, remember that the park is named Blue Spring and not Springs.

47

IGNORE THE SPEED LIMIT
AT K1 SPEED DAYTONA

Race your indoor go-kart at speeds up to 45 miles per hour at K1 Speed Daytona, located in the shadows of Daytona International Speedway. Sure, it's a far cry from the 200 miles per hour reached on the high banks, but remember, you are inside a building, piloting a 20-horsepower, zero-emission, electric go-kart. Junior karts are available for kids who are at least 48 inches tall, but parents and kids can't race at the same time unless children meet the adult height requirements, 58 inches tall. Junior and adult karts are not allowed on the track at the same time due to safety guidelines. So strap on your helmet and get ready for 12 laps of hair-raising adventure as you navigate through turns, straightaways, and elevation changes on your way to the checkered flag. Did all that speed give you an appetite? Stop off at the Paddock Lounge and enjoy delicious pub-style food and drinks. No drinking and driving allowed.

2455 W International Speedway Blvd., Ste. 300, 386-400-9848
k1speed.com/daytona-location.html

SERVE UP AN ACE
AT PICTONA PICKLEBALL

"Pictona—where pickleball is more than a game—it's a lifestyle" says all you need to know about this location. For pickleball enthusiasts, Pictona is where the action is. Billed as the third-largest pickleball facility in Florida and completed in 2022 at a cost of more than $14 million, this massive facility features 49 courts, 13 of which are covered to protect players from the brutal summer heat and fast-moving afternoon showers central Florida is known for. All courts are fenced to help prevent interference from other courts. The Championship Court features seating for up to 1,200 spectators during tournaments. Pictona amenities include two player shops, a restaurant, a nine-hole putting green, cornhole, shuffleboard, croquet, and table tennis. No matter your skill level, you are welcome at Pictona. Lessons are available for newcomers to the game, but be prepared—the action can get heated on the courts.

1060 Ridgewood Ave., Holly Hill, 386-310-7067
pictona.org

LET THE WIND BLOW THROUGH YOUR HAIR
AT DESTINATION DAYTONA

Destination Daytona is the center of Bike Week and Biketoberfest in Daytona Beach. The centerpiece of Destination Daytona is Teddy Morse's Daytona Harley Davidson. At well over 100,000 square feet, to say this place is massive is an understatement. Whether you are new to bike culture and want riding lessons, or are a grizzled veteran looking to trade your ride, Daytona Harley Davidson can help. If you are looking for a new or used bike, factory-authorized maintenance and repairs, or just an officially licensed T-shirt, it's worth the short drive.

Destination Daytona is more than Harley Davidson. Make the Clarion Inn your Bike Week home. Multiple dining options, from fast food to sit-down service, are available. Shopping, while mostly biker related, can help you spend an afternoon. Or maybe you'll be able to attend a concert at the 5,000-seat pavilion that has played host to acts such as Molly Hatchet, Travis Tritt, and Candlebox. Also, be sure to check our list of the best biker bars and really get into the traditions of Bike Week.

1637 N US Hwy. 1, Ormond Beach, 386-671-7100
daytonaharleydavidson.com

50

CRUISE THE BEACH ON AN E-BIKE
FROM DAYTONA ELECTRIC BIKES

Take that long bike ride on the sands of Daytona Beach without all the pedaling. You can see the sites at your own pace because these e-bike rentals are by the hour. Maybe you haven't ridden a bike in years and are afraid of being a bit rusty. Try one of the e-trikes. These three-wheelers offer a higher level of stability with the same ease of use. Don't worry about needing a helmet or lock; Daytona Electric Bikes has you covered. Stop for lunch with no worries. Speaking of worries, if you break down or get a flat tire, roadside assistance is available during normal business hours. If you already own an e-bike, Daytona Electric Bikes can provide any servicing your bike may need. Ask for a no-obligation quote. So, get to pedaling. Or rather, don't pedal, but get out on an e-bike and see Daytona Beach.

116 Dunlawton Ave., Ste. 4, Daytona Beach Shores, 386-214-2452
daytonaelectricbikes.com

TIP

Once you try an e-bike, you are likely to become a convert. If you fall in love with your ride, let the staff at Daytona Electric Bikes know. They can apply your rental fee toward the purchase of a brand-new e-bike.

PLAY WHERE THE PROS PLAY

AT LPGA INTERNATIONAL

Featuring 36 holes over two courses designed by golf legends Arthur Hills and Rees Jones, these courses challenge even the best players. The courses are so respected that LPGA International is the home course of the Ladies Professional Golf Association and serves as host to the final stage of LPGA Qualifying School. The Hills course measures just under 7,000 yards from the farthest men's tees, while the Jones course comes in at 7,100 yards. Courses feature water hazards, sand bunkers, undulating greens, and, at times, quite narrow fairways. Both courses are rated four-star by the prestigious *Golf Digest*. Amenities include short-game and putting-green practice areas. Want to improve your game? LPGA and PGA professionals are available for private lessons. The clubhouse features the best local pro-shop for all your gear needs as well as Malcom's Bar & Grill. Members have exclusive access to a fitness center and swimming complex.

1000 Champions Dr., 386-274-5742
lpgainternational.com

TIP

While membership has its privileges, you do not have to be a member to play the LPGA International courses. Book your date and tee time online to be assured of playing these high-level courses.

PACK YOUR CLUBS WHEN VISITING DAYTONA BEACH

The Club at Venetian Bay

63 Airport Rd., New Smyrna Beach, 386-424-5775
venetianbaygolf.com

Daytona Beach Golf Club

600 Wilder Blvd., 386-671-3500
daytonabeachgc.com

Oceans Golf Club

2 Oceans West Blvd., Daytona Beach Shores
386-788-2998
oceansgolfclub.com

The Preserve at Turnbull Bay

2600 Turnbull Estates Dr., New Smyrna Beach
386-427-8727
thepreserveatturnbull.com

Riviera Country Club

500 Calle Grande St., Ormond Beach, 386-677-2464
rivcc.com

Spruce Creek Country Club

1900 Country Club Dr., Port Orange, 386-756-6116
sprucecreekclub.com

Victoria Hills Golf Club

300 Spalding Way, DeLand, 386-738-6000
victoriahillsgolf.com

52

CREATE YOUR OWN LEGEND

PLAYING PUTT-PUTT AT MULLIGAN'S LAGOON

The legend of Ace Mulligan is multi-faceted. Maybe he was a surfer, but he might have been a pro golfer. He could have been a treasure hunter or a retired philosophy professor. Some claim he discovered the Fountain of Youth. After you play 18 holes of mini golf, you can make up your own legend for how this tropical oasis came to be located beachside in Daytona Beach Shores. Here, you will find a perfect location for a selfie with a shark, discover Ace's plane, putt your way through a cave. Discover waterfalls, tiki torches, and surfboards while the waves of the Atlantic Ocean crash in the background. After sinking your putts, join the family at the on-site pizza pub and enjoy a delicious pizza and snacks. There are plenty of options for the kids, and adult beverages available for adults. Enjoy a rest on the patio chairs by the firepit while the kids play cornhole. Mulligan's Lagoon is a gnarly wave of fun for the entire family.

2504 S Atlantic Ave., Daytona Beach Shores, 386-310-4242
mulligranslagoon.com

PAY RESPECTS TO CHIEF TOMOKIE

AT TOMOKA STATE PARK

The fish-filled waters around what is now Tomoka State Park were once home to the Timucuan Native American village called Nocoroco. During the 1760s, much of the area was acquired by the Scottish merchant Richard Oswald. His 20,000-acre holding was known as Mount Oswald Plantation, with enslaved Africans growing indigo, rice, cotton, and sugar. Today Tomoka State Park offers visitors hiking trails, fishing, boating, picnicking, 100 pet-friendly campsites with RV hook-ups, and wildlife viewing. You might see birds, deer, gopher tortoises, snakes, alligators, manatees, and (if you are lucky) an elusive bobcat. Bird-watchers make Tomoka State Park home during annual migration periods, when more than 160 species of birds have been observed. While there, be sure to pay your respects to the mythical Chief Tomokie, whose fictional legend is told through a 45-foot-tall sculpture created by artist Fred Marsh in 1957.

2099 N Beach St., Ormond Beach, 386-676-4050
floridastateparks.org/tomoka

SWING FROM THE TREES
AT DAYTONA BEACH ZIPLINE ADVENTURE

Located in picturesque Tuscawilla Park, Daytona Beach Zipline Adventure is where you can harness up and climb ladders, cross wooden bridges, walk tightropes, and zip-line from tree to tree at heights of up to 45 feet and spanning distances of up to 500 feet in length. Choose from the easier Course One, with 10 obstacles and four zip lines, or opt for one of the combo packs, where you will also challenge Course Two, with up to 24 obstacles and six zip lines. Are you a college student, school faculty or administrator; active or retired military; or a first responder? Bring your ID and inquire about discounts on the Full Combo package. Safety monitors are on hand making sure everyone is safe and secure while gliding through the trees. Be mindful of the weather, though, as the frequent Central Florida rains can shut down the zip lines on a moment's notice.

1000 Orange Ave., 386-882-8016
facebook.com/DaytonaBeachZipline

TIP

After soaring through the trees, be sure to stop and see the World War I memorial located in Tuscawilla Park. Dedicated in 1932, the memorial was originally located in what is now the Riverfront Esplanade before being moved to its current location.

55

HANG TEN
AT THE JIMMY LANE SURFING ACADEMY

New Smyrna Beach is often called the World's Safest Bathing Beach (there's even a local AM radio station with the call letters WSBB) or the Shark Bite Capital of the World. Either way, the Atlantic Ocean beckons visitors and locals alike—and seriously, encounters with sharks are extremely rare. If you want to ride the waves, there's no better place to learn than the Jimmy Lane Surfing Academy, where the ocean is your classroom and the waves are your lessons. Former professional surfer Jimmy Lane and his team offer private lessons, group classes, and summer camps. Don't have your own board yet? No problem—rentals are available. You will often find the Jimmy Lane Surfing Academy bus on the hard-packed sands with students of all ages in tow. No matter your age or level of experience, Jimmy Lane can help you become a better surfer and get more enjoyment out of this quaint little beach town.

New Smyrna Beach, 386-314-1356
surf-lane.com

TIP

In addition to having been a professional surfer and surf-school owner, Jimmy Lane is also an accomplished artist. Jimmy can often be found on Saturdays outside the New Smyrna Museum of History with his easels, brushes, and paints, creating and talking with passersby.

56

PUT ONE FOOT IN FRONT OF THE OTHER

AT REED CANAL PARK

Located between the busy Nova Road and Ridgewood Avenue, Reed Canal Park offers a free, tranquil retreat where residents and visitors alike can get a welcome respite from life's pressures. Reed Canal Park offers 35 acres full of recreational facilities. Walk the shell hiking trail, play disc golf, enjoy lunch at the pavilion and picnic facilities, bring the kids to the barrier-free playground, or allow man's best friend to run free at one of two dog parks. Sit and watch the turtles in the small lake, or maybe bring your rod and reel and try your luck. Enjoy watching visitors who bring their model boats to the calm waters. Bird-watchers will be able to spy a great variety of feathered friends. While there are plenty of shaded areas, particularly on the disc golf course, bring your water bottle and sunscreen because much of the park is open.

2871 S Nova Rd., South Daytona, 386-322-3070
southdaytona.org/topic/subtopic.php?topicid=23&structureid=18

TIP

As you walk the hiking trail, you will come across a sign marking the approximate location where, a 13-foot, three-to-five-ton, giant ground sloth roamed the area 130,000 years ago. Today this incredibly rare and nearly complete fossil, which was discovered at Reed Canal Park in 1975, may be seen on display in the Prehistory of Florida Gallery, located at the Museum of Arts & Sciences, only a short drive away on Nova Road.

CATCH AND RELEASE
WITH BOB STONEWATER'S TROPHY BASS GUIDE SERVICE

For nearly 50 years, Bob Stonewater has been one of the leading guides on the St. Johns River, Lake Rousseau, the Suwannee River, and numerous other bass-fishing waters. His service is so successful that he has been featured on ESPN, *Bill Dance's Outdoors*, *Florida Sportsman*, and many other print and video features. *In-Fisherman* TV editor Steve Quinn stated he had never caught as many lunker bass, weighing seven to 10 pounds, in a day as he did with Bob. While Bob has hung up his guiding rod and reel, the family business continues under the careful guidance of Bob's nephew, Captain Jim Pratt. Captain Jim is no rookie to the St. Johns and other bass haunts. He grew up fishing the rivers and worked as a guide for Stonewater's for more than four years. He knows where the fish are. Bring your fishing license and get ready to catch some fish.

386-279-9436
bobstonewater.com

CAST YOUR LINE WITH A PROFESSIONAL FISHING GUIDE

Captain Sean's Daytona Beach Fishing Trips

386-547-1456, daytonabeachfishingtrips.com

Ferg's Guide Service

321-439-5476 or 321-439-5096, fergsguideservice.com

Finomenal Fishing Guide

386-753-7572, finomenaladventures.com

Fisher's Lagoon Charters

386-290-0786, fisherslagooncharters.com

Lucky Spot Charters

386-444-0049, luckyspotcharters.com

NSB Shark Hunters

386-235-5573, nsbsharkhunters.com

Rare Breed Charters

386-295-4581, rarebreedcharters.com

Sea Spirit Fishing

386-763-4388, seaspiritfishing.com

Sudden Strike Offshore Adventures

407-314-3355, suddenstrikeoffshoreadventure.com

Three Lagoon Fishing Charters

321-794-3182, threelagoonfishingcharters.com

Vulcan Charters

386-405-0651, facebook.com/VulcanCharters

SOAR WITH THE EAGLES
AT SKYDIVE DELAND

If jumping out of an airplane from an altitude of nearly 14,000 feet is on your bucket list, you are in luck. Since 1982, Skydive DeLand has been serving jumpers of all experience levels, from those making their very first tandem jump to those with hundreds of jumps to their credit. Safety is of the highest importance. Jumpers receive instructions and all necessary equipment, including special protective goggles if you wear glasses. After training, enjoy your 12-minute flight to altitude and get ready for a 60-second drop at speeds up to 120 miles per hour before your professional tandem partner deploys the parachute for a five-minute descent to the safety and stability of Mother Earth. If you want to relive your jump, or prove to friends and family you actually did it, hire the onsite professional videographer to record your feat.

1600 Flightline Blvd., DeLand, 386-738-3539
skydivedeland.com

TIP

While you are at the DeLand Municipal Airport, be sure to visit the DeLand Naval Air Station Museum. This small, volunteer-operated museum has some incredible aircraft on exhibit and always has new projects going. The building itself is listed on the National Register of Historic Places. Visit and learn more about the role DeLand played in training pilots for World War II.

SCORE A PERFECT 10
AT DAYTONA ICE ARENA

Some cold-weather sports are no longer exclusive to northern states. Florida has jumped into the world of hockey with two skates. The Tampa Bay Lightning and the Florida Panthers hockey teams have each won multiple Stanley Cups and draw strong nightly attendance, proving the sport is just as popular in Florida as in Canada. Ice-skating rinks throughout Florida are flourishing, and one of the best is Daytona Ice Arena. Whether you are just getting on skates and looking for lessons or are an expert skater and want to play competitive hockey, you can do it here. Want to try it out before investing in expensive skates? You can rent skates and skate-aid scooters to help get you up on your blades. If the physical activity takes its toll, skate on over to Celly's Sports Pub for some great pub-style food and sports on their nine large screens.

2400 S Ridgewood Ave., Ste. 63D, South Daytona, 386-256-3963
daytonaicearena.com

TAKE IN OCEAN VIEWS FROM HIGH ABOVE

AT DAYTONA BEACH PARASAIL

Have you ever seen the flocks of pelicans flying over the ocean and wondered what it must be like? Head over to Daytona Beach Parasail and find out what these majestic birds see and hear. Arrive early to review and sign your waiver. After a brief safety orientation riders are strapped into their harnesses, and then the fun begins. The crew, including a Coast Guard–licensed captain, will take you on a boat ride from the security of solid ground, where up to three riders at a time will be attached to a winch-powered parasail and prepped for takeoff. During your approximately six-minute flight, at full height you will be soaring 600 to 1,000 feet above the Atlantic Ocean. Be prepared for amazing views of Daytona Beach you'll never forget. Are you with friends but not wanting to take to the skies? No problem—for a small riding fee, you can join on the boat to be a firsthand witness to the fun.

4936 S Peninsula Dr., Ponce Inlet, 386-547-6067
daytonaparasail.com/home

TIP

While at Daytona Beach Parasail, check out their sister companies, which offer Jet Skiing, fishing charters, and ecotours. A full day on the ocean awaits.

STROLL WITH YOUR PUPPY ON VOLUSIA COUNTY'S DOG-FRIENDLY BEACHES

The hard-packed sands of the Daytona Beach area shouldn't be for human enjoyment only, and the Volusia County Council has provided several areas where you can take your dog with you as you walk the beach. Three sections of beach have been dedicated for dog use: Lighthouse Point Park in Ponce Inlet, Smyrna Dunes Park in New Smyrna Beach, and the area from Rockefeller Drive to Milsap Road in Ormond Beach. Here dogs can play and enjoy the ocean with a few simple rules for their human companions to obey. Humans must be kept on a leash no longer than six feet long. Humans and their dogs are not permitted in dedicated wildlife areas and are not allowed to harass or interact with wildlife. And finally, owners should be responsible and clean up after their pet. Dogs love the great outdoors. The sounds, smells, and feel of the beach are a perfect way to exercise your dog and stimulate their mind. A tired dog is a happy dog!

Volusia County Beach Services, 386-239-7873
volusia.org/services/public-protection/beach-safety/dogs-on-beach.stml

SCORE A TOUCHDOWN
WITH THE BETHUNE-COOKMAN UNIVERSITY WILDCATS

Continuing a 100-year-long tradition, the Bethune-Cookman University Wildcats football team proudly represents Daytona Beach in the Southwestern Athletic Conference in the Division I Football Championship Subdivision. The Wildcats play their home games in Daytona Stadium, which always features enthusiastic crowds. The highlight of each season is when the Wildcats clash with in-state rivals the Florida A&M University Rattlers in the Florida Classic Game, held each year in Orlando. The matchup is so storied that it annually draws a national television broadcast. The halftime battle of the bands is as anticipated as the on-field action. Highlights on the home schedule each season include homecoming and Senior Appreciation Day, which draw crowds full of family and former Wildcats.

The Wildcats have produced more than 30 National Football League players including Hall of Fame member Larry Little. Little was an undrafted offensive guard who played for the Chargers before earning his reputation playing for the Miami Dolphins.

640 Dr. Mary McLeod Bethune Blvd., 386-481-2215
bcuathletics.com/sports/football

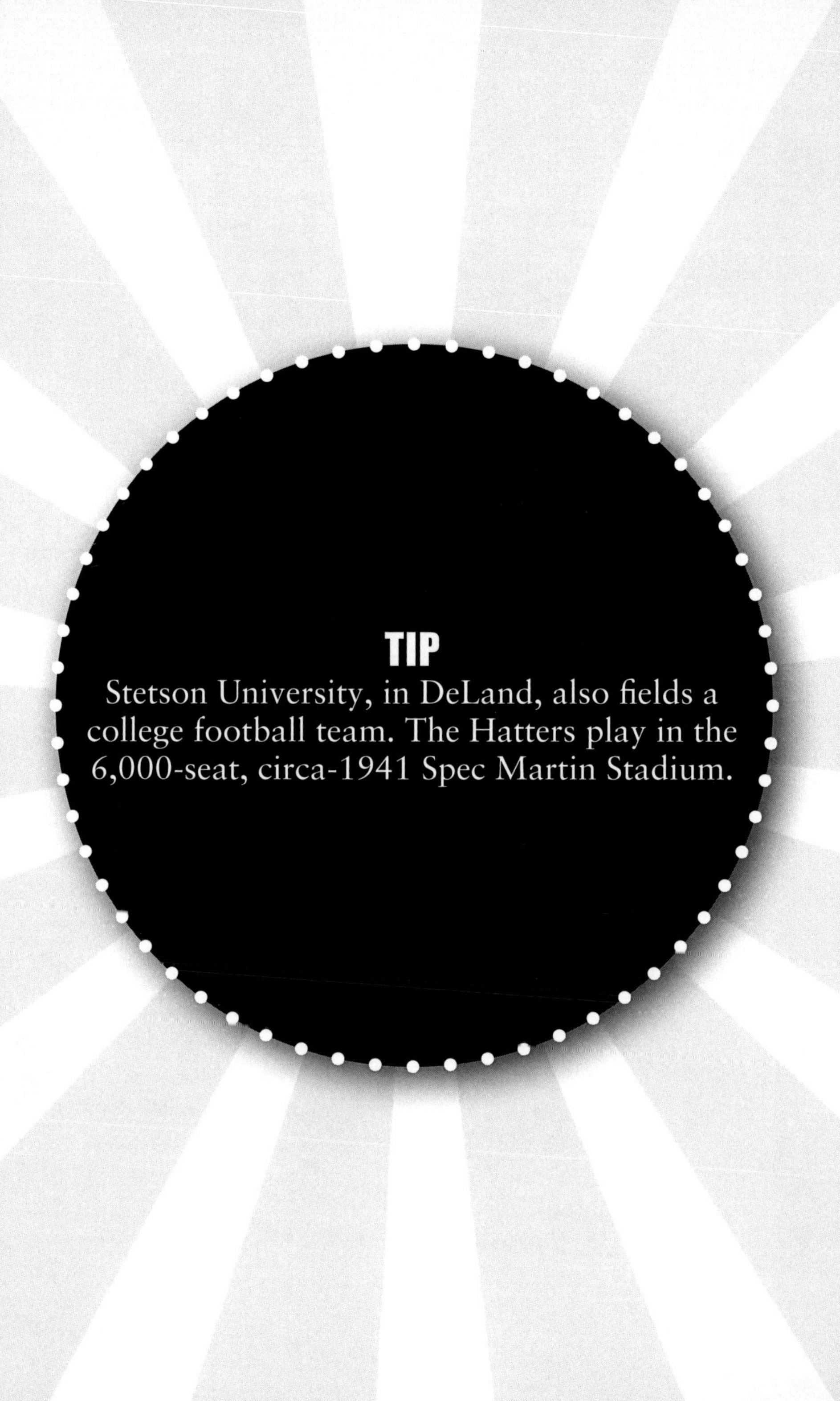
TIP
Stetson University, in DeLand, also fields a college football team. The Hatters play in the 6,000-seat, circa-1941 Spec Martin Stadium.

RACE FOR THE CHECKERED FLAG
AT DAYTONA INTERNATIONAL SPEEDWAY

Join 100,000 of your closest friends and root for your favorite driver at the World Center of Racing. Opened in 1959, Daytona International Speedway (DIS) is now home to the biggest race of the NASCAR year, the season-opening Daytona 500. DIS is not only NASCAR, however. The 24 Hours of Daytona kicks off "Speedweeks" each year. Motorcycle races, car shows, concerts, and Magic of Lights, the largest Christmas light show in Volusia County, are held here. Take a guided track tour, have your photo taken with the most recent car to win the Daytona 500, and visit the Motorsports Hall of Fame of America. No visit is complete without a close-up look at the statue of "the Intimidator," Dale Earnhardt.

1801 W International Speedway Blvd., 800-748-7467
daytonainternationalspeedway.com

TIP

A fun way to see if you measure up to your racing heroes is to take the Daytona 500 Champions Walk of Fame, located outside the speedway entrance. Beginning in 1996 with Dale Jarrett, each Daytona 500 winner has placed their hands, right foot, and autograph in a three-foot-by-three-foot block of cement that is later installed when the drivers are back in town for the August race.

DISCOVER RACING HISTORY

Birthplace of Speed Park

21 Ocean Shore Blvd., Ormond Beach, 386-676-3250
ormondbeach.org/Facilities/Facility/Details/16

Daytona Memorial Park

The final resting place of Bill France Jr., Fireball Roberts, Marshall Teague, and Ray Fox
1425 Bellevue Ave., 386-262-1311
daytonamemorialpark.com

New Smyrna Speedway

3939 FL–44, New Smyrna Beach, 386-427-4129
newsmyrnaspeedway.org

Racing's North Turn

4511 S Atlantic Ave., Ponce Inlet, 386-322-3258
northturnemail.wixsite.com/my-site-1

Smokey Yunick Marker

Near 241 Riverside Dr.
hmdb.org/m.asp?m=229022

Streamline Hotel

140 S Atlantic Ave., 386-947-7470
streamlinehotel.com

Volusia Speedway Park

1500 FL–40, De Leon Springs, 386-985-4402
volusiaspeedwaypark.com

Dunlawton Sugar
Mill Gardens

CULTURE
AND HISTORY

64

CLIMB 203 STEPS
TO THE TOP OF PONCE INLET LIGHTHOUSE

Put on your step tracker and climb the 203 steps to the top of Ponce Inlet Lighthouse, where unrivaled views await. Opened in 1887, the lighthouse was in continuous operation until 1970 when the United States Coast Guard deactivated the tower. The tower was reactivated in 1982 and continues to be operated by museum staff. On-site you can see keeper's dwellings, a lens exhibit showcasing just how complicated these lights can be, and a fascinating display of Cuban refugee rafts. The small Woodshed Theater shows a 20-minute film outlining the history of the lighthouse and is a must-see. If you intend to climb to the top, remember, you must go back down those same 203 steps.

Located just a few yards away from the lighthouse is the Constance D. Hunter Historic Pacetti Hotel Museum. Here, you will be whisked back to an 1880s fishing resort and boardinghouse that served visitors from all over the country who flocked to the well-stocked seas and rivers of the area.

4931 S Peninsula Dr., Ponce Inlet, 386-761-1821
ponceinlet.org

TIP

For those with an extreme interest in lighthouse history, a visit to Edgewater-New Smyrna Cemetery should be on your to-do list. Here you will find the final resting spot of William R. Rowlinski, the first Principal Keeper of the Mosquito Inlet Lighthouse, now known by the more tourist-friendly name Ponce Inlet.

VISIT THE "RETREAT"

AT THE MARY McLEOD BETHUNE HOME

Mary McLeod Bethune is without question one of the most influential women in the history of Florida. So important is her legacy that she has been commemorated in Statuary Hall at the United States Capitol. Today, visitors can tour the home that has often been referred to as the "Retreat." Docents will guide you through many rooms in the home still decorated with the personal belongings of Dr. Bethune and, provide information about the home itself, the story of the legendary Black Rose, and the many elephants found throughout. They will share stories of famous visitors such as Jackie Robinson, Langston Hughes, and Eleanor Roosevelt. Gifts from luminaries such as John D. Rockefeller adorn the home. The home received designation as a National Historic Landmark.

Before leaving, visit the grave of Dr. Mary McLeod Bethune located adjacent to the home.

640 Dr. Mary McLeod Bethune Blvd., 386-481-2121
cookman.edu/mmbhome/index.html

CELEBRATE BLACK HISTORY

African American Museum of the Arts

(see the Noble "Thin Man" Watts Amphitheater across the street)
325 S Clara Ave., DeLand, 386-736-4004
africanmuseumdeland.org

Bethel AME Church

210 E Howry Ave., DeLand, 386-736-2324
facebook.com/betheldeland

DeLand Memorial Hospital and Veterans Museum

230 N Stone St., DeLand, 386-490-6204
delandhouse.com/deland_memorial_hospital_museum

Freemanville Historic Site

3431 S Ridgewood Ave., Port Orange, 386-506-5501
hmdb.org/m.asp?m=45453

Howard Thurman Home

614 Whitehall St., 386-258-7514
howardthurmanhome.com

Mary McLeod Bethune Beach Park

6656 S Atlantic Ave., New Smyrna Beach
386-423-3300 ext. 18072
www.volusia.org/services/public-works/coastal-division/coastal-parks/mary-mcleod-bethune-beach-park.stml

Mary S. Harrell Black Heritage Museum

314 N Duss St., New Smyrna Beach, 386-478-1934
blackheritage.org

Mt. Bethel Baptist Institutional Church

700 S Martin Luther King Jr. Blvd., 386-255-6922
mtbethelbaptist-daytonabeach.com

PUT ON YOUR 10-GALLON HAT
AND TOUR THE STETSON MANSION

Completed in 1886, the Stetson Mansion bills itself as "The House that Hats Built," a clever reference to original homeowner John B. Stetson's legacy as a hatmaker. Stetson, an early snowbird and benefactor to Stetson University, spared no expense in creating what is considered one of the grandest pre-20th-century homes in Florida—and the first home built in the state with Edison electricity. From inlaid parquet floors to more than 10,000 panes of glass, the restored and updated mansion glows. Today, the mansion is a private residence, but the owners open it for public tours during winter and spring. The mansion is closed from June through October. From November through mid-January, the home is awash in holiday decor that would turn Scrooge into a fan.

1031 Camphor Ln., DeLand, 386-785-3961
stetsonmansion.com

TIP

Any visit to DeLand must include a walking tour of Stetson University. Enjoy serene, tree-lined grounds and visit pre-20th-century buildings still used by students today. Stop by the Homer and Dolly Hand Art Center and the Gillespie Museum. Follow with a short stroll to downtown DeLand shops and restaurants.

67

SUMMON GHOSTLY SPIRITS AT CASSADAGA SPIRITUALIST CAMP

Originally formed as a winter spiritualist camp in 1894 by George P. Colby, a medium from New York, Cassadaga Spiritualist Camp consists of 57 acres with 55 homes, plus assorted other buildings. Spiritualism combines philosophy and religion. Nearly 40 mediums and 30 spiritual healers are available in Cassadaga for appointments. Courses, workshops, and historical walking tours of the camp are available, as well as a well-stocked gift shop in the welcome center. If you want to get back to nature, head over to the county-owned Colby-Alderman Park and enjoy paved and unpaved trails, a fishing dock, a playground, and picnic tables. Interpretive signage will help explain the historic elements of the park.

Cassadaga Spiritualist Camp Welcome Center
1112 Stevens St., Cassadaga, 386-228-2880
cassadaga.org

TIP

Consider booking a room at the Hotel Cassadaga. This hotel was constructed in 1927 and offers Reiki healing, séances, lectures, and courses on topics of a spiritual nature. Whether you are staying on-site or just visiting the town, a meal at Sinatra's Ristorante is recommended. Don't miss their dueling pianos.

LEARN ABOUT 19TH-CENTURY SUGAR PLANTATIONS

AT DUNLAWTON SUGAR MILL GARDENS

Today, we take sugar for granted, finding it readily available at the grocery store. At the Dunlawton Sugar Mill Gardens, visitors can see the monumental effort required to process sugarcane during the 19th century. Large machinery, once operated by enslaved and animal labor, sits amongst the ruins of coquina and brick structures underneath a modern canopy, allowing visitors to stay out of the Florida sun. Interpretive panels throughout provide background on what visitors are seeing and how the machinery worked. The site was once home to a roadside attraction called Bongoland, which showcased a Seminole Indian village, live animals, and dinosaur figures created from concrete and chicken wire. Some of the dinosaurs are still standing and are a favorite for children. As you walk the trails, admire the gardening work throughout the park accomplished by a local volunteer group. Find the sundial and give it a try. It works!

950 Old Sugar Mill Rd., Port Orange, 386-736-5953
https://dunlawtonsugarmillgardens.org/index.html

VISIT THESE ADDITIONAL SUGAR MILLS

Bulow Plantation Ruins

3501 Old Kings Rd., Flagler Beach, 386-517-2084
floridastateparks.org/parks-and-trails/bulow-plantation-ruins-historic-state-park

New Smyrna Beach Sugar Mill Ruins

600 Mission Dr., New Smyrna Beach, 386-736-5953
volusia.org/services/community-services/parks-recreation-and-culture/parks-and-trails/park-facilities-and-locations/historical-parks/sugar-mill-ruins.stml

Three Chimneys

715 W Granada Blvd., Ormond Beach, 386-677-7005
ormondhistory.org/the-three-chimneys-sugar-works

DISCOVER DAYTONA'S EARLIEST RESIDENTS
AT PINEWOOD CEMETERY

Active since 1887, Pinewood Cemetery, located across from the Boot Hill Saloon at the corner of Main St. and Peninsula Ave., is the final resting place to more than 1,700 of Daytona Beach's earliest residents and their descendants. Those wandering the peaceful rows of headstones will find the burial location of members of the United States Congress, Union and Confederate Civil War veterans, and Charles Burgoyne, a prominent local businessman, politician, and philanthropist, whose name you will find throughout Daytona Beach. One person whose remains will not be found here is Matthias Walter Day Jr. the namesake of Daytona Beach. He is interred in Mansfield Cemetery, in Mansfield, Ohio.

Pinewood Cemetery, while peaceful in atmosphere, can be a struggle to walk. There are elevation changes, soft sand, above-ground tree roots, and flat headstones, necessitating caution while walking. Closed-toed shoes are a safety must.

Corner of Main St. and Peninsula Dr.
findagrave.com/cemetery/72459/pinewood-cemetery

SOME OTHER DAYTONA BEACH CEMETERIES TO EXPLORE

Daytona Memorial Park

1425 Bellevue Ave., 386-262-1311
daytonamemorialpark.com

Edgewater-New Smyrna Cemetery

700 S Ridgewood Ave., Edgewater
386-320-5999
edgewater-newsmyrnacemetery.com

Hillside Cemetery

215 Seton Trail, Ormond Beach, 386-217-0868
hillsidecemeteryormondbeach.org

Mount Ararat Cemetery

1427 Bellevue Ave.
findagrave.com/cemetery/72286/mount-ararat-cemetery

Oakdale Cemetery

800 N Clara Ave., DeLand, 386-734-0626
findagrave.com/cemetery/72371/oakdale-cemetery

Pilgrim's Rest Cemetery

791 W Granada Blvd., Ormond Beach
findagrave.com/cemetery/2178774/pilgrims-rest-cemetery

GIVE THANKS
AT THE TOURIST CHURCH

Only a town as unique as Daytona Beach could have a church that is known by the nickname the "Tourist Church." The Seabreeze United Church of Christ building was constructed in 1929 under the direction of architect Harry Griffin. The nickname dates to around 1913, when many of the winter worshippers were tourists. The church became affiliated with the United Church of Christ in 1964. The building is primarily constructed of solidified marl stone, commonly called "bog rock," which looks like coquina but is distinct. Also unique to the building are the large stained-glass windows depicting the Nativity. The large pipe organ was manufactured by Visser-Rowland and is one of only 20 in the state. This unusual example of Mission Revival architecture helped place the church on the National Register of Historic Places in 1995. Regular services are still held weekly, and tourists are always welcome.

501 N Wild Olive Ave., 386-252-6314
seabreezeunitedchurch.org

SAY YOUR PRAYERS AT UNIQUE CHURCHES

All Saints Episcopal Church

155 Clark St., Enterprise, 386-668-4108
facebook.com/allsaintsenterprise

Basilica of Saint Paul Roman Catholic Church

317 Mullally St., 386-252-5422
stpauldaytona.org

Daytona Beach Drive-In Christian Church

3140 S Atlantic Ave., 386-767-8761
driveinchurch.net

First United Methodist Church

115 E Howry Ave., DeLand, 386-734-5113
firstchurchdeland.org

Grace Episcopal Church and Guild Hall

4110 S Ridgewood Ave., Port Orange, 386-767-3583
egracepo.org

Mt. Bethel Baptist Institutional Church

700 S Martin Luther King Jr., Blvd., 386-255-6922
mtbethelbaptist-daytonabeach.com

St. Mary's Episcopal Church

216 Orange Ave., 386-255-3669
stmarysdaytona.org

St. Rita's Colored Catholic Mission

Now home to Mary S. Harrell Black Heritage Museum
314 N Duss St., New Smyrna Beach, 386-478-1934
blackheritage.org

71

PRESERVE, ADVOCATE, AND EDUCATE

AT HALIFAX HISTORICAL MUSEUM

Chartered in 1949, the Halifax Historical Society is the oldest local historical organization in Volusia County. Today, the museum is housed in the County of Volusia–owned Merchants Bank building that dates to circa 1910. The building, listed on the National Register of Historic Places, is one of the most important pieces of architecture in Daytona Beach. The museum exhibits an eclectic collection of items, including those associated with locals who have served in the military, automobile and motorcycle racing, lifeguards, Jackie Robinson, and a local's wall of fame. The museum also has a collection of research materials including documents, maps, and photos. One of the most unique stories told by the museum is that of Brownie, the Town Dog. Brownie was a stray dog living in the downtown area who was loved by locals. Brownie had a bank account opened in his name to cover vet bills. A monument to Brownie, where his remains were buried, can be found in the Riverfront Esplanade. Today, visitors can take home their own stuffed Brownie the Town Dog from the museum as a souvenir.

252 S Beach St., 386-255-6976
halifaxhistorical.org

STUDY LOCAL HISTORY AT SMALL, LOCAL MUSEUMS

DeLand House Museum (West Volusia Historical Society)

137 W Michigan Ave., DeLand, 386-740-6813
delandhouse.com

DeLand Naval Air Station Museum

910 Biscayne Blvd., DeLand, 386-738-4149
delandnavalairmuseum.org

Flagler Beach Historical Museum

207 S Central Ave., Flagler Beach, 386-517-2025
fbmflagler.wixsite.com/flagler

Holly Hill History Museum

1065 Daytona Ave., Holly Hill, 386-252-2339
hollyhillhistoricsociety.com

Mary S. Harrell Black Heritage Museum

314 N Duss St., New Smyrna Beach, 386-478-1934
blackheritage.org

New Smyrna Museum of History

120 Sams Ave., New Smyrna Beach, 386-478-0052
nsbhistory.org

Ormond Beach Historical Society

38 E Granada Blvd., Ormond Beach, 386-677-7005
ormondhistory.org

Ponce Inlet Historical Museum

143 Beach St., Ponce Inlet, 386-761-2408
ponceinlet.org/tour-explore/our-town/ponce-inlet-historial-museum

72

WALK IN THE FOOTSTEPS OF JOHN D. ROCKEFELLER
AT THE CASEMENTS

Walk through the Casements, and you will quickly understand why Standard Oil tycoon John D. Rockefeller just had to purchase the property in 1918. Named for the large casement windows throughout the home, the Casements served as Rockefeller's winter home from 1918 until his death in 1937. Vacant for many years, the property was purchased by the city of Ormond Beach in 1974 and restored by 1979. No visit to the Casements is complete without seeing the art and native costumes in the Hungarian Folk Exhibit. Today, the property is on the National Register of Historic Places and serves as a cultural center with special exhibits, self-guided tours, movies on the grounds, children's events, music festivals, yoga classes, and more.

25 Riverside Dr., Ormond Beach, 386-676-3216
thecasements.net/index.html

TIP

The Ormond Beach Celtic Festival, held each spring, features music, dancing, a whiskey tasting, Highland games demonstrations, traditional foods, and heritage groups to help you trace your lineage. So put on your finest kilt and make plans to attend the biggest Celtic Festival in Volusia County.

SERVE UP JUSTICE
AT THE HISTORIC VOLUSIA COUNTY COURTHOUSE

Constructed during the late 1920s at the then-astounding cost of $500,000, the Historic Volusia County Courthouse would cost many times that amount to build today, even if you could find artisans able to recreate the detailed work. The exterior features fluted Corinthian columns, vaulted arches, and a distinctive copper-clad dome that towers above its surroundings. The building's elaborate twin facades allow entry from both the north and the south. The interior showcases amazing tile work, twin marble staircases, a fountain, and above, a stained-glass dome. Be sure to take in the Art in Public Places collection of paintings, collages, and photographs throughout. Climb the stairs and view the original courtroom, and while there be sure to look above and see the segregated seating used during the Jim Crow era. Today, the courthouse is home to county offices but is accessible to the public.

125 W New York Ave., DeLand
hmdb.org/m.asp?m=136023

TIP

Just outside the courthouse is Chess Park. Walk through the tree-lined park, find the large chess mural, and be sure to notice the chess piece–shaped architecture.

VALOR RESTS
AT CAPE CANAVERAL NATIONAL CEMETERY

As one of only five national cemeteries in the state of Florida, Cape Canaveral National Cemetery holds a special place in the minds and hearts of veterans and their families. After many years of requests, Congress authorized $2.1 million for the purchase of 318 acres in Brevard County for the creation of the cemetery. When the cemetery was opened for interments in January 2016, it was estimated there was space for 17,000 gravesites, including casket and cremains. Those eligible for burial include veterans or service members, their spouses, and certain dependent family members. The cemetery is open to visitors daily from sunrise to sunset.

Notable burials include Flight Officer Edwin T. Cowan, a member of the Tuskegee Airmen; James Rollins Eddy, who served in the United States Air Force as an intelligence officer in Korea and Japan before serving four terms in the Florida House of Representatives; and Director of the Navy Nurse Corps, Rear Admiral Alene B. Duerk.

5525 US Hwy. 1, Mims, 321-383-2638
cem.va.gov/cems/nchp/capecanaveral.asp

THANK A VETERAN IN VOLUSIA COUNTY

DeLand Memorial Hospital and Veterans Museum

230 N Stone St., DeLand, 386-490-6204
delandhouse.com/deland_memorial_hospital_museum

DeLand Naval Air Station Museum

910 Biscayne Blvd., DeLand, 386-738-4149
delandnavalairmuseum.org

Deltona Veterans Memorial Park and Museum

1921 Evard Ave., Deltona, 386-789-8247
vmpm.weebly.com

Ormond Memorial Art Museum & Gardens

78 E Granada Blvd., Ormond Beach, 386-676-3347
ormondartmuseum.org

Ponce Inlet Veterans Memorial

Davies Lighthouse Park, Ponce Inlet
ponce-inlet.org/307/Ponce-Inlet-Veterans-Memorial

Veterans Memorial Plaza and Tom Staed Veterans Memorial Bridge

Orange Ave.
volusia.org/veteransmemorialbridge/memorial-plaza.stml

Veterans Museum and Education Center

302 Vermont Ave., 386-256-7909
vmaec.org

EXPLORE THE INDIAN RIVER LAGOON AT MARINE DISCOVERY CENTER

With a stated mission "to protect our coastal ecosystems through education, conservation, and exploration," the Marine Discovery Center has risen from humble beginnings in 1997 to the thriving organization it is today. The Marine Discovery Center plays a key role in protecting and reinvigorating vital local ecosystems. Today, visitors can see marine aquariums featuring fish, snails, crabs, turtles, and more. Interactive exhibits educate visitors about these creatures. Tour the native wildflower and butterfly gardens. Maybe take one of the nature trails or launch your kayak into the river. Perhaps the most popular draws are the ecotours, where you might see sea turtles, manatees, dolphins, roseate spoonbills, pelicans, ospreys, and the occasional bald eagle.

520 Barracuda Blvd., New Smyrna Beach, 386-428-4828
marinediscoverycenter.org

TIP

Don't confuse the Marine Discovery Center with the county-operated Marine Science Center located in Ponce Inlet. The MSC, whose focus is on seabird and sea turtle rehabilitation, is also worth a visit, especially if you are already visiting the Ponce Inlet Lighthouse.

LEARN TO PAINT, PLAY GUITAR, OR SPEAK A FOREIGN LANGUAGE

AT THE HUB ON CANAL

Since its opening in 2012, the HUB on Canal has been a cultural meeting place for people of all interests and backgrounds. For creatives of all stripes, there is always something going on at the HUB. For artists, they offer classes and gallery exhibitions. Are you a musician? They offer regular jam sessions, performances, and open mic nights. Want to learn a foreign language, join a book club, or maybe purchase art directly from an artist? Stroll into the HUB and make it happen. The HUB offers youth camps and courses designed specifically for young creatives. Join them on the first Saturday of each month for special events.

132 Canal St., New Smyrna Beach, 386-957-3924
thehuboncanal.org

TIP

Be sure to stop by Jane's Art Center, located around the corner on Downing Street, where you can learn everything you ever wanted to know about pottery and working in clay. If you enjoy the HUB on Canal, consider visiting Gateway Center for the Arts in DeBary. They provide a similarly wide range of offerings, from courses to gallery space to live performances.

VISIT A 19TH-CENTURY SPORTSMAN'S PARADISE

AT DEBARY HALL

Stepping on to the DeBary Hall Historic Site property is to be taken back to the late 1800s: a time when Florida was still undeveloped; a time when the wealthy would arrive by train or steamship; a time when Frederick deBary, an agent for Mum's Champagne, owned more than 5,000 acres of land near Lake Monroe. Now operated by the County of Volusia, visitors can tour the mansion and see other outbuildings. Regular programs including line dancing lessons, story time, high tea, "Lemonade Lectures," and more are offered in the reconstructed barn. Don't miss the special holiday-themed evening events at Halloween and Christmas, hosted by costumed docents.

198 Sunrise Blvd., DeBary, 386-668-3840
volusia.org/services/community-services/parks-recreation-and-culture/parks-and-trails/park-facilities-and-locations/historical-parks/debary-hall-historic-site

TIP

Tours of the mansion include a visit to the second floor. For visitors unable to climb the stairs, video offerings of the second-floor exhibits are available, allowing all visitors to enjoy the full DeBary Hall experience.

STROLL "AMERICA'S MAIN STREET"

WHILE TAKING THE DELAND MURAL WALK

DeLand has frequently been recognized for its downtown revitalization efforts. It was one of the first Florida communities to receive a Main Street America award, and was a national ranking survey's 2017 "America's Main Street" winner. Today, the sidewalks along Woodland Avenue are full of locals, visitors, and students from nearby Stetson University shopping in locally owned stores or getting a bite to eat at one of the many restaurants and cafés that line the street. Many are also taking in the large number of street art pieces that are to be found. The DeLand Mural Walk features 15 murals located throughout the downtown area that help highlight local history for visitors. An online guide will help visitors find all the murals. Topics include important local residents, historic businesses, nature, and more. Put on your walking shoes and find them all.

Downtown DeLand
mainstreetdeland.org/mural-walk

TIP

Be on the lookout for pieces of sculpture, wrapped utility boxes, and the Rufus Pinkney mural. Pinkney operated a shoeshine stand in DeLand for the better part of 60 years and became a local legend.

TOUR A SMITHSONIAN-CALIBER MUSEUM

AT THE MUSEUM OF ARTS & SCIENCES

Who says you have to visit a major metropolitan area to find a world-class museum? You can do that right in Daytona Beach at the Museum of Arts & Sciences. For those interested in science, the Lohman Planetarium is an incredible stop before viewing the Prehistory of Florida gallery. African art, exhibits of weapons and armor, and one of the best collections of Cuban art in the United States can be found here. Decorative and American art can be seen in other galleries, while the "Visible Storage Building" is a unique look at pieces not currently in a traditional exhibit. The Root Family Museum contains Coca-Cola memorabilia, while the train station exhibit is a favorite for kids of all ages. Speaking of kids, take them to the Williams Children's Museum for an interactive experience they will love. End your visit at the Cici and Hyatt Brown Museum of Art, featuring the largest collection of Florida art in the world.

352 S Nova Rd., 386-255-0285
moas.org

TIP

Are you a Volusia County resident? Visit the museum on the first Tuesday of each month, show your local ID, and visit for free.

ART LOVERS WILL DELIGHT IN LOCAL OFFERINGS

African American Museum of the Arts

325 S Clara Ave., DeLand, 386-736-4004
africanmuseumdeland.org

Atlantic Center for the Arts

1414 Art Center Ave., New Smyrna Beach, 386-427-6975
atlanticcenterforthearts.org

Homer and Dolly Hand Art Center

On the campus of Stetson University
139 E Michigan Ave., DeLand, 386-822-7270
handartcenter.org

Museum of Art - DeLand

100 N Woodland Blvd., DeLand, 386-734-4371
moartdeland.org

Ormond Memorial Art Museum & Gardens

78 E Granada Blvd., Ormond Beach, 386-676-3347
ormondartmuseum.org

Southeast Museum of Photography

On the campus of Daytona State College
1200 W International Speedway Blvd., 386-506-3894
southeastmuseumofphotography.org

DISCOVER YESTERDAY TODAY AT BARBERVILLE PIONEER SETTLEMENT

The saying "everything old is new again" may not apply to Barberville Pioneer Settlement. Tracing its roots to the mid-1970s, the settlement is a field trip destination for Volusia County school children. Visitors learn the struggles that early Florida residents encountered. Exhibits include a blacksmith shop, print shop, carriage house, post office, church, railroad depot, and more. Many buildings are not original to the site but have been painstakingly relocated from their original sites, retaining a high level of authenticity. Annual events such as the Fall Jamboree feature folk musicians, arts and crafts vendors, living history demonstrations, and tours. While the settlement is a bit off the beaten path, a visit is a reminder of how far we have come, and perhaps a reminder of what we have left behind.

1776 Lightfoot Ln., Barberville, 386-749-2959
pioneersettlement.org

TIP

A tourist attraction in its own right, the Barberville Yard Art Emporium features unique, handmade oddities. From a gigantic eagle to outdoor tables made from teak, decorative yet functional Mexican ceramics, and cast-aluminum statues, you will find it located just minutes from the Pioneer Settlement.

WALK A LONG STRETCH OF COASTLINE AT CANAVERAL NATIONAL SEASHORE

Canaveral National Seashore encompasses more than 58,000 acres and 24 miles of pristine, undeveloped beach. Indigenous tribes including the Ais and Timucuan can be traced back approximately 5,000 years on the property. Archaeologists have mapped more than 100 shell middens, or refuse piles, the most famous being Turtle Mound, accessible via a hiking trail. The 50-foot-high mound is approximately two-thirds its original size, having been reduced in the 19th and early 20th centuries by the removal of shells in the creation of early railroad beds and roadways. Today visitors can view the Eldora State House, the former home of artist and activist Doris Leeper. Leeper was also instrumental in the establishment of the Doris Leeper Spruce Creek Preserve, named in her honor, and the Atlantic Center for the Arts. The seashore offers an ideal viewing location for day launches from Kennedy Space Center. Leashed dogs are welcome lagoon-side but are not allowed on the beach or the boardwalks.

Apollo Visitor Center
7611 S Atlantic Ave., New Smyrna Beach, 386-428-3384
nps.gov/cana/index.htm

Atlantic Sounds

SHOPPING AND FASHION

GET YOUR GROOVE ON
AT ATLANTIC SOUNDS

For more than 40 years, Daytona Beach has been home to one of the most eclectic record stores you will ever find: Atlantic Sounds. When owner Mike Toole received the Jan & Dean album *Ride the Wild Surf* as a gift while a child, he never could have foreseen that it would lead to his 60,000-plus pieces of vinyl inventory today. Visitors to the shop may be greeted by Iron Maiden playing but will find a selection to suit any taste. Shoppers vary from longtime, serious, well-heeled collectors looking for rarities to those seeking the newest Record Store Day limited releases, to newcomers to the format maybe seeking out their favorite top-40 singers. Toole has seen trends come and go, and for those who still favor the sound and convenience of compact discs, he offers a large selection. Whether you are seeking records that are new or used, modern or vintage, common or rare, Atlantic Sounds probably has it.

138 W International Speedway Blvd., 386-258-1420
facebook.com/atlanticsoundsvinyl

FIND YOUR DREAM RIDE
AT HANKSTERS HOT RODS

The premium collector car market is hot, fueled by nostalgia and television shows such as *Counting Cars*, *Fast N' Loud*, *Car Master: Rust to Riches*, and others. If you remember a certain car from your youth, or have ever wanted to own a muscle car, head to Hanksters. Whether your choice is a hot rod, a muscle car, or maybe even a vintage motorcycle, the team can put you behind the wheel. With more than 30 years of experience, owner Gary Hankinson has been buying, building, restoring, and selling classic vehicles his entire adult life. From 1960s classics to the growing early 2000s truck and SUV market and from Mustangs to vans, Hanksters has them, or can acquire and restore them for you, all with their buyer satisfaction guarantee. Visit their showroom to see the current inventory, or maybe just purchase a T-shirt. Hanksters is located in the building that had been home to the circa-1972 Skate City roller-skating rink, and they have retained the hardwood floor as part of their showroom.

Do you have a classic vehicle to sell? Hanksters is always purchasing high-quality classic cars.

1790 S Nova Rd., South Daytona, 386-944-9219
hanksters.com

TIP

Hanksters has a second showroom in Homer City, Pennsylvania.

DISCOVER THE OUT OF THE ORDINARY

AT THE POSH PINEAPPLE

Owner Cheryl Lorenz's love of pineapples and all they symbolize—ideals such as hospitality and friendship—helped lead her to her business's name, the Posh Pineapple. Today, shoppers can find a wide array of unique home, gift, and clothing items and brands that won't be found at every other store. Whether you are looking for a baby shower item, cards, holiday items, or decorative pieces for your home, you can find it at the Posh Pineapple. Are you seeking to upgrade your wardrobe and put a stamp on your own personal style? The Posh Pineapple can help with dresses, active wear, and accessories such as jewelry and handbags that will set you apart from everyone else. Is your purchase a gift? Have it wrapped in the store's signature lime green, black, and white gift wrap to make it even more unique. Stop in and see why the store bills itself as a "unique and trendy boutique gift shop."

330 Canal St., New Smyrna Beach, 386-427-7674
poshpineapplensb.com

TIP

Make an afternoon of your visit to Canal Street. Start with lunch at one of the many restaurants, and then stroll up and down the street, enjoying the many locally owned shops selling antiques, flowers, clothing, olive oil, candles, furniture, and more.

LET YOUR DOG "CHEWS" WHAT'S NATURAL

AT CHEWS WILD

Feeding your four-footed best friend as nutritiously as you feed yourself is important. Many over-the-counter dog foods are full of preservatives and dyes that are harmful to animals. Chews Wild looks to educate pet owners and supply the finest in natural foods and chews, ensuring that your dogs, whether large or small, lead the healthiest life possible. Performance-based dry foods in a variety of brands and flavors are available. Not sure what your dog might like? Let them try a sample. If your dog has food allergies, Chews Wild can find the perfect food for them. Natural treats from a variety of protein sources including lamb, duck, rabbit, venison, and more are available. Is your pup a chewer? Instead of rawhide, try long-lasting elk antlers or beef cheek rolls. Whether you have a puppy new to your home or a senior dog, these all-natural foods and treats will benefit them.

600 S Yonge St., Unit 5B, Ormond Beach, 386-243-5336
chewswild.square.site

TIP

Can't make it during their regular business hours? Visit them at the Port Orange Farmers Market or one of the many pop-up events they attend throughout the area. Bring your dog!

CATCH BIG WAVES
AT DAYTONA BOARD STORE SURF SHOP

Owner Todd Ayres has been catching big waves since he was a boy of only 6. At age 18, he headed to California where he entered the world of professional surfing. His success led him to open Oceanside Surf and Sport in California before returning to Florida where he opened Daytona Board Store surf shop in 2011. Today, Daytona Board Store remains locally owned, operated, and staffed. They offer more than 50 brands of surfboards to surfers of all experience levels. Not ready to commit to purchasing a board? Try renting different styles of board to find what is best for you. Are you a novice or want to improve your skills? Sign up for their Daytona Surf Camp. Daytona Board Store also offers skateboards, boogie boards, and related apparel from the most popular brands. Stop in and get all your beach accessories, then go catch a wave.

2044 S Atlantic Ave., Daytona Beach Shores, 386-256-4951
daytonaboard.store

HIT THE BEACH AT A SURF SHOP

Bikini Company

142 E Granada Blvd., Ormond Beach, 386-492-4070
bikinicompany.com

Maui Nix Surf Shop

Multiple locations
717 N Atlantic Ave., 386-253-1234
mauinix.com

Red Dog Surf Shop

801 A1A, New Smyrna Beach, 386-423-8532
reddogsurfshop.com

Ron Jon Surf Shop

Multiple locations
4151 N Atlantic Ave., Cocoa Beach, 321-799-8820
ronjonsurfshop.com

Salty Dog Surf Shop

100 S Atlantic Ave., 386-253-2755
saltydogsurfshop.com

Surf Station

1020 Anastasia Blvd., St. Augustine, 904-471-9463
surfstationstore.com

FIND EVERYTHING YOU NEED AT DAYTONA FLEA & FARMERS MARKET

Do you need a doodad, a whatchamacallit, or a thingy? You'll find it at Daytona Flea & Farmers Market. From regular garage-sale-type vendors to fine jewelry to automobile tires, it can be had here. Put on your comfortable walking shoes and be prepared to examine nearly 300 vendors under the roof, not including those set up outside. If you are looking for the finest, locally grown produce at budget-friendly prices, head to Aisle P South, where the produce vendors are set up. All that walking and bargaining might make you hungry, so be sure to seek out the Snack Shack locations throughout. For car enthusiasts, the first Saturday of each month features a Classic Car Cruise-In with more than 300 vehicles on display. Do you feel really daring? Head to the south parking lot, where you'll find Leading Edge Helicopter Tours. Flights of various lengths are available, providing a unique vantage point from which to see Daytona Beach.

1425 Tomoka Farms Rd., 386-253-3330
daytonafleamarket.com

START YOUR DAY ON THE WATER AT NEW SMYRNA OUTFITTERS

The waters around Daytona Beach offer incredible fishing opportunities. To make the most of a day on the lake, river, or ocean, you need the right gear and the pros at New Smyrna Outfitters can provide everything you need. Whether you are a novice or an experienced angler, the friendly and knowledgeable staff will make sure you leave satisfied. Seeking a fly rod or maybe something heavy duty for ocean adventures? They have it in stock and a reel to go with. Don't forget tackle. They stock inshore, offshore, and fly lures. With the latest technology and most popular brands in stock, you'll be ready to catch your limit. You can't hit the water without proper protective apparel. The Florida sun will chew you up. Whether you need outerwear for children, men, or women, New Smyrna Outfitters has it in your size. Conveniently located on Canal Street, look for the large marlin above the entrance. After visiting, you might just catch one this large.

223A Canal St., New Smyrna Beach, 386-402-8853
newsmyrnaoutfitters.com

89

BUY AND SELL
AT DUNN'S ATTIC

The Dunn family name is familiar to longtime locals for their businesses in fields such as lumber, toys, and hardware. Since 2013, Dunn's Attic has been a local leader in upscale consignment and auction services. Their 28,000-square-foot showroom features more than 30,000 items. Specialties include antiques and collectibles, jewelry, art, and gently used furniture and home decor items. In addition to consignment and local auction services, Dunn's offers online auctions, a firearms store, and several specialized Etsy shops, and they can even manage your estate-sale needs. Because of the sheer size of Dunn's, plan to take a couple of hours for your visit. With that in mind, stop off at Rosie's Café, their on-site restaurant and home of the $1 mimosa. Breakfast, lunch, and dessert are available. Sample the old-fashioned soda fountain with more than 180 flavor combinations available. Did I mention the $1 mimosa?

136 W Granada Blvd., Ormond Beach, 386-673-0044
dunnsattic.com

TAKE HOME A LIFETIME SOUVENIR

FROM WILLIE'S TROPICAL TATTOO

Tattoos are hardly the sole domain of bikers, musicians, and sailors. They have been in the mainstream for years, with everyone from students to CEOs decorating their bodies with permanent markings. This permanent art may be strictly decorative or have deeper meaning, such as commemorating a loved one. Maybe you would like to remember your visit to Daytona Beach. If so, head over to Willie's Tropical Tattoo and let their talented artists turn your wish into art you will wear for a lifetime. Located in the same building for more than two decades, Tropical Tattoo has experienced artists who will work with you to customize your design. Whether you are looking for a new design, a portrait, or a coverup, the professionals at Tropical Tattoo are committed to your 100 percent satisfaction. Willie's is a member of the major industry organizations and upholds the highest standards in health, safety, and cleanliness.

825 S Yonge St., Ormond Beach, 386-672-1888
tropicaltattoo.com

91

DISCOVER ARTISAN PRODUCTS
AT WILD OATS & BILLY GOATS

Located in the former Little Drug Store–Victoria Theater building on Canal Street, Wild Oats & Billy Goats is a staple in the arts scene of New Smyrna Beach. Whether you are redesigning your home's interior, looking for truly unique gift items, or browsing for handmade products, Wild Oats & Billy Goats will become one of your preferred destinations. Artisans offer everything from one-of-a-kind pottery and fashionable jewelry to homemade soaps, candles, and other products that will turn your home into a personal oasis. Stop in and discover this unique shopping opportunity. If you're an artist, check their website to find out how to "join the herd."

412 Canal St., New Smyrna Beach, 386-957-4325
wildoatsandbillygoatsnsb.com

TIP

Longtime locals will be glad to tell you how the lunch counter at Little Drug was more than a place to get lunch or ice cream; it was a place for business meetings and social gatherings. It was a throwback to a slower, simpler time. Today, the concept has been revived through the updated Little Griddle on Canal, which shares the building with Wild Oats. Stop in for breakfast or lunch, and treat yourself to a milkshake or sundae.

WORK OR PARTY IN FASHION
FROM SKIP'S WESTERN OUTFITTERS

For more than 40 years, Skip's Western Outfitters has provided the best in functional and fashionable western wear to Florida residents. From origins at a Sunday flea market stall, to a small store in Osteen, to a superstore in Daytona Beach, Skip's reputation has grown, and they are a trusted source for first responders, bikers, outdoor enthusiasts, and, of course, those who prefer western fashion. If you are looking for boots for working on the farm or going to the club, Skip's should be your first stop. Whether you prefer crocodile, python, ostrich, or other leathers, Skip's has it. It's not just boots, either. If you need a cowboy hat, belt, jeans, or maybe a flirty dress, you'll find it. Don't forget to bring the kids. There's a whole line of children's apparel for the little cowboy or cowgirl in your life.

1900 W International Speedway Blvd., #100, 386-255-0455
skipsboots.com

STRIKE UP THE BAND
AT TOTAL ENTERTAINMENT MUSIC STORE

In a town full of creatives with dozens of outlets for sharing that creativity, it's natural for there to be an amazing independent musical instrument store nearby, and Total Entertainment Music Store is just that. Whether you are just starting to callous your fingers on a guitar or bass, are building endurance in your hands and arms on a drum set, or are simply an avid musician looking for a new toy, Total Entertainment is your best stop. Maybe you want that new guitar you laid eyes on in a popular magazine, or you want a vintage axe—acoustic or electric. Either way, the expert staff can get it for you if it isn't already in stock. Need a new amp? No problem, they have dozens in stock. Drum sticks, heads, cymbals, pedals, and more are all waiting for you. Keyboards, high school band needs, and musical accessories of every type are available at Total Entertainment Music Store, located conveniently on International Speedway Boulevard—just look for the amazing guitar mural on the side of the building. You may already have a musical instrument, but you don't have these instruments.

501 W International Speedway Blvd., 386-254-8727
facebook.com/TotalEntertainmentMusicStore

94

IGNITE YOUR CHILD'S CREATIVITY
AT OLIVER AND GRAY

Oliver and Gray give parents options that go beyond the standard children's line of cookie-cutter clothing and plastic toys, offering a carefully curated selection of items featuring natural fibers and heirloom-quality craftsmanship. From baby items to fashionable early-childhood shirts, pants, and dresses, your child will look and feel great in these clothes. For play time they offer an array of plush, felt, wooden, and musical toys guaranteed to keep your young child occupied and engaged. A fun collection of books will help you and your child bond while instilling a lifelong love of reading. The store features a full calendar of events, from kids' yoga to sensory play-station days to kids' crafting events. Whether you want something for your child, a gift, or a baby shower, Oliver and Gray will help you discover just what you are looking for.

109 W Indiana Ave., DeLand, 386-473-1672
oliverandgray.com

PAMPER YOURSELF
AT THE SPA AT RIVERVIEW

Whether you are an overnight guest at the 140-year-old Riverview Hotel, a day-tripper, or a local resident, a day of relaxation and pampering can be had at the Spa at Riverview. Situated next to the 18-room boutique hotel, the Spa offers the finest in relaxation and recharging services. From Swedish massage to hot-stone massage to targeted deep-tissue massage, the trained experts will leave you invigorated and ready to face the day. Body treatments, facials, manicures, and pedicures are all offered. If you are looking for the perfect birthday, anniversary, or holiday gift for your partner, purchase a gift certificate for a couple's massage and enjoy together. Make it a truly special visit with a Riverview Spa breakfast or lunch. You won't find better beignets this side of New Orleans.

Are you a regular spa visitor? Join the loyalty program and earn points redeemable toward future spa services.

103 Flagler Ave., New Smyrna Beach, 386-424-6262
riverviewhotel.com/spa

TIP

In order to provide the most relaxing and peaceful atmosphere possible, spa staff request that cell phones be left in your room or secured in your car, or at a minimum that ringers be turned to silent or vibrate. Just sit back, relax, and enjoy.

REMODEL YOUR HOME WITH RECLAIM

FROM RELICS & RUST

OK, it's a bit of a drive, but when you see the quality and beauty of reclaim architectural salvage that owner Terry Swearingen provides, you'll agree it was worth the trip. Terry often spends his days salvaging history, whether in the form of flooring, joists, rafters, doors, hinges, chandeliers, or windows from old homes that would otherwise fall to the wrecking ball. You can often find video updates of demolition projects, items for sale, and completed renovations on the store's Facebook page. Give it a follow to keep up. If you are a professional decorator, this will become your second home. Are you considering opening a themed bar or restaurant? Let Relics & Rust fulfill your dreams. Start that renovation project today.

Store is open by appointment only.
Ocklawaha, 352-537-4441
relicsandrustantiques.com
facebook.com/people/Relics-Rust/100063573504750/#

SWAP OUT THAT BORING WARDROBE
AT VON MODE VINTAGE

Are you in the market for a whole new look? Maybe you have a retro-themed party on your entertainment calendar but don't have the right look in your closet. Look no further than downtown DeLand and Von Mode Vintage. From authentic garments to classic reproductions from the 1920s through the 1960s, they have it. Women's dresses, skirts, swimwear, jewelry, shoes, and more are all available. Men, Von Mode Vintage hasn't forgotten you. From formal suits to blazers, shirts, caps, and accessories, you'll wow her in these vintage fashions. Getting married and want a unique ceremony? Ask about vintage-inspired bridal wear. Your ceremony will be one that isn't soon forgotten when you walk down the aisle in a vintage gown. Do you need alterations on vintage clothing you already own? Von Mode Vintage can help. Do you have vintage clothing and accessories you'd like to sell? Get in touch. The store's inventory is always changing, and your items may be on the racks soon.

106 S Woodland Blvd., Ste. B, DeLand, 407-496-8555
vonmodevintage.com

ELEVATE YOUR CULINARY SKILLS
AT THE ANOINTED OLIVE

If you are looking to expand your culinary skills, the Anointed Olive can help you out. From premium olive oils and infused oils to the finest in aged balsamic vinegars, your taste buds are going to explode when you add these to your family recipes or to one of the many easy-to-follow recipes on the website. Try the garlic-infused olive oil with your favorite crusty breads. That may be your entire meal. Looking to make your own charcuterie board? The Anointed Olive has a large selection of specialty foods that will meet your needs. If you need something for the gourmand in your life, gift sets of all types are available. The friendly staff will guide you to the perfect selection. With more than 30 varieties of extra-virgin olive oil and more than 35 flavor-infused balsamic vinegars in stock, there is one for every palate.

240 N Nova Rd., Ormond Beach, 386-333-9236

118 N Woodland Blvd., DeLand, 386-873-8123
shop.theanointedolivellc.com

TIP

One visit and you'll be back again and again, so join the loyalty program and earn redeemable points for every dollar spent.

HAVE MORE FUN THAN A BARREL OF MONKEYS
AT BARREL OF BOOKS AND GAMES

Located in tranquil and cozy downtown Mount Dora, Barrel of Books and Games has been the locally owned shop where residents and visitors have fed their need for reading and playtime for more than a decade. It was formerly located in the town's old police station, but the success of the business necessitated a new location. Now readers can find thousands of titles, from *New York Times* bestsellers to hard-to-find nonfiction, at the newly expanded location, still in the heart of Mount Dora. As their name says, it's not just about books. Whether you are looking for a classic game for the family or maybe a Mount Dora jigsaw puzzle, they have it. Don't see what you are looking for? Special orders are easily available.

Be sure to keep your eyes open while you're there. You might just find Page, the cat, hiding on a bookshelf. Page has quickly become a Facebook favorite, as followers try to find her hiding spot in posted photos.

403 N Donnelly St., Mount Dora, 352-735-1950
barrelofbooksandgames.com

OPEN YOUR MIND BY READING A GOOD BOOK

Abraxas Books

256 S Beach St., 386-307-6478
www.facebook.com/p/Abraxas-Books-100063988184088

The Family Book Shop

1301 N Woodland Blvd., DeLand, 386-736-6501
familybookshopdeland.com

Fern and Fable Books

51 W Granada Blvd., Ormond Beach, 386-299-5526
fernandfablebooks.com

Maya Books and Music

204 E 1st St., Sanford, 407-321-6504
facebook.com/p/Maya-Books-and-Music-100063759302317

The Muse Book Shop

112 S Woodland Blvd., DeLand, 386-734-0278
facebook.com/people/The-Muse-Bookshop

Novel Tea Book Shop

150 Tomoka Ave., Ormond Beach, 386-317-6820
www.novelteabookshop.com

Spellbound Bookstore

105 N Oak Ave., Sanford, 321-578-7418
spellboundbookstore.net

Turtle & Bea Book Boutique

2146 S Riverside Dr., Ste. 7, Edgewater, 386-566-8364
facebook.com/p/Turtle-Bea-Book-Boutique-61565223342697

AMAZE YOUR FRIENDS WITH TRICKS FROM DAYTONA MAGIC

With origins in New Jersey, Daytona Magic has been in business locally since 1976, selling magic- and clown-related supplies of all types. Whether you are an experienced magician looking to upgrade your stage presence or are just starting out, they have tricks and gags that meet your skills, experience, and budget. They offer more than 3,600 different card effects. Try some sleight of hand with Money Magic. For advanced magicians there is a deep line of fire and flash tricks, guaranteed to astound any audience. For children just starting out, Daytona Magic stocks a full line of age- and skill-appropriate tricks, allowing youngsters to build their skills and confidence. Many of the supplies and tricks at Daytona Magic are created in one of their in-house carpentry shops or their sewing shop. Daytona Magic sells to both retail and wholesale accounts, thus spreading the magic of Daytona Beach around the globe.

1360 N US Hwy. 1, Ste. 105, Ormond Beach, 386-252-6767
daytonamagic.com

TIP

Each November, Daytona Magic hosts an incredible convention, the Daytona Beach Festival of Magic, which attracts hundreds of magic enthusiasts, including some of the biggest names in the field.

ACTIVITIES BY SEASON

SPRING

SUMMER

FALL

WINTER

SUGGESTED ITINERARIES

FAMILY FUN

ON THE WATER

HAVE FUN WHILE EXERCISING

DATE NIGHT

ADRENALINE

RAINY DAY

TIME FOR YOURSELF

Baci Pizzeria Ristorante